BOONE COUNTY LIBRARY

2040 9100 14 542 6

D0006061

HOW TO TRIM SAILS

623.8813   Schweer, Peter.
schw   How to trim sails

17.95

BOONE COUNTY PUBLIC LIBRARY
FLORENCE. KY 41042

SCHEBEN BRANCH   DEMCO
          AUG 0 7 1997

HOW TO
TRIM SAILS
—— Peter Schweer ——

SHERIDAN HOUSE

BOONE COUNTY
1145126

This edition first published 1991
by Sheridan House Inc.
Dobbs Ferry, NY 10522

Reprinted 1994, 1995, 1996

© Klasing & Co Gmbh

© English Language text Nautical Books 1990

Translated from the German Edition by
Robin Inches, MITI.

Photographs: Hans-Gunter Kiesel (3),
Peter Schweer

Drawings: Peter Schweer

All rights reserved. No part of this
publication may be reproduced, stored
in a retrieval system or transmitted
in any form or by any means, electronic,
mechanical, photocopying, recording or otherwise,
without the prior permission in writing of the
Publishers.

Printed in Great Britain

ISBN 0–924486–23–6

Contents

Why this 'trimming primer'?   8

Basics and Introduction to Trimming Sails   11

Trimming Controls for the Mainsail   17
Main Halyard. 17
Main Boom Kicking Strap 20
Luff Tensioner (Cunningham) 26
Clew Outhaul. 28
Reefing 30
Main Sheet and Leech 31
Leech Line 33
Sail Battens 36
Tell-tales Along the Leech 36
The Topping Lift 38
The Traveller. 39

Trimming Controls for the Headsail   42
Headsail Halyard 42
Forestay 42
Sheet Leads 46
Barber Hauler 55
Tell-tales 57
The Leech Line 60
The Sail Foot 60

Correct Camber   61

Mast Rake   64

Weather Helm – Causes and Cures   68

Trim for Beating 72
Light Airs. 72
Medium Strength Winds. 74
Strong Winds. 75

Trim for Reaching 78
Light Airs. 78
Medium Strength Winds. 79
Strong Winds. 80

Trim for Running 81
Light Airs. 81
Medium Strength Winds. 82
Strong Winds. 82

Masthead Rig 84
Basic Trim of the Mast 86
Light Airs Trim. 88
Medium Strength Wind Trim 88
Strong Wind Trim 89

The ⅞ or Fractional Rig with Swept-back Spreaders 90
Basic Trim of the Mast 91
Light Airs Trim. 93
Medium Strength Wind Trim 94
Strong Wind Trim 94

The ⅞ or Fractional Rig with Running Backstays 96
Basic Trim of the Mast 99
Light Airs Trim 100

Medium Strength Wind Trim   101
Strong Wind Trim   102

Dinghy Rig with Swept-back Spreaders   103
Mast Section 104
Spreaders   105
Rig Tension   105
Kicking Strap 106
Mast Control 107
Mainsheet Angle of Pull   110
Basic Trim of the Mast 110
Light Airs Trim 111
Medium Strength Wind Trim   112
Strong Wind Trim 113

Ordering a New Mainsail   116

Trimming Tables   117
Masthead Rig – Beat   117
Masthead Rig – Reach 118
Fractional Rig with Swept-back Spreaders – Beat   119
Fractional Rig with Swept-back Spreaders – Reach   120
Fractional Rig with Running Backstays – Beat   121
Fractional Rig with Running Backstays – Reach   122
Dinghy Rig – Beat   123
Dinghy Rig – Reach 124

Index   125

Why this 'trimming primer'?

I have written this book for sailors who respect sailing in its traditional form, and for those who may develop a degree of sporting ambition. It is for those aiming to sail their dinghy or yacht swiftly to the next port-of-call, making best use of the sails and taking sensible account of the prevailing conditions.

This 'trimming primer' is intended to appeal primarily to those skippers and crew members who fidget nervously on the cockpit thwart or the side deck if another boat comes up from astern and draws ahead slowly to windward — or worse, to leeward.

Cruising sailors who occasionally want to take part in a club regatta will find comprehensive advice in the form of trimming instructions about the correct basic trim, and proven tips for changing it as wind and wave conditions change. Real racers will be able to look up tested trimming refinements and tricks going well beyond the basics.

I have gathered together the trimming experience acquired over the past 35 years as the skipper of the most varied types of boats — from 'Pirates' to 12-Metre yachts; it could be as many as 600 boats. I have intentionally avoided using any formulae, diagrams and specific figures because I do not want to give the impression that this is a scientific treatise. That sort of thing is justified for static investigations in wind tunnels and towing tanks; I, on the other hand, have attempted to express myself in the easy-to-understand fashion to which I have become accustomed from a multitude of rig-trimming demonstrations at boat shows. Trimming sails is an art, not a science; it is that art which has to be acquired. That also defines the object of this book: I should like to make the art of trimming sails more attractive for you — without the ballast, and without the need to buy expensive extras for your boat. Every piece of trimming advice can be used in practice, using only the running rigging normally available on the boat.

One of the essentials on board a sailing or auxiliary yacht is to set the sail cambers correctly. (Almost) continuous scrutiny of the sails and of the wind angle of incidence should be just as much second nature as the frequent check in the rear-view mirror when driving a car. Strictly speaking, there is only one camber per sail that is correct for any given set of conditions, whose parameters are wind strength, angle of attack, and seaway pattern; the art of sail trimming, in effect, consists of adjusting the sail to match as nearly as possible the presumed ideal shape. A basic knowledge of aerodynamics is as useful in this connection as experience gained from speed comparisons with other boats.

I must emphasize that just reading this book is not enough; what it contains must also be put into practice. So do not just push this trimming primer into the bookcase in your drawing room — it belongs on board. Only there, combining the theory with practical application, can success be achieved.

Finally, I want to record my thanks to all my friends and acquaintances who have allowed me to sail with them, and from whom I have learnt how to trim rigs and sails: Ralf Steckhan, Bernie Beilken, Ulli Libor, Hans Otto Schümann, Rodney Pattisson and, above all, Adje Hauschildt. The book also contains trimming experience gained during various 'Happy Racing' race-training demonstrations in the Mediterranean, by looking over the shoulders of Vincent Hösch, Peter Nowka, Willy Kuhweide and Wilfried Schomäker. Many stimulating comments have reached me from boat-show visitors during my rig-trimming demonstrations; many questions put to me there have helped to fashion this book to meet the requirements of those who sail.

Peter Schweer

Every halyard and tensioner, even the spinnaker boom downhaul and topping lift, is led back to the cockpit. However, there are some jammers that cannot be operated from there, being located too far for'd on the deck.

Basics and Introduction to Trimming Sails

Successful trimming of a boat is dependent not only on the know-how of the crew, but also on the range of trimming gear. The sheets, halyards and outhauls must be:
- clearly arranged
- easy to reach
- free-running
- undamaged

A snakes' honeymoon of unsorted rope can easily lead to a tangled knot forming and jamming a halyard. A recipe for chaos! For that reason some yachts carry around a large knife lashed to the mast foot — just in case. To avoid the risk of jamming, all lines involved should be laid out clearly and unmistakably, well before the initiation of any manoeuvre.

Cordage that is all the same colour can lead to uncertainty in its handling; it is all too easy to grab the end of the wrong rope. To ensure identification, therefore, it is worthwhile using variously coloured or marked ropes.

If the trimming gear is complex, or if there are frequent crew changes, clear identification — particularly of the jammers on the coach roof — is essential. Perfect for this are felt-pens with water-

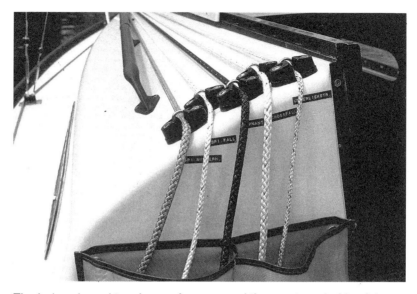

The halyards and tensioners from around the mast are led back to the cockpit. On small boats there is no need for a winch for setting up. The cam cleats can be clearly identified by means of Dymo tape; the ends of the lines disappear into practical stowage bags. Differing colour cordage helps to avoid mix-ups.

proof ink. The inscription can later be removed using methylated spirit or a polishing liquid.

Important trimming controls such as headsail and main sheets, primary sheets, main boom kicking strap, traveller and standing backstay, should be operable from the windward side. This applies principally to dinghies and smaller yachts, where the crew sits on the side deck to keep the boat as upright as possible. Any weight removed from the windward side may adversely affect the speed. Obviously trimming is efficient only if the equipment is easy to operate; chafed lines, skewed blocks and unfavourably located winches can easily cause problems. Accordingly, every piece of trimming gear must be positioned and designed so that even in

A good arrangement of halyards and tensioners turned towards the cockpit. The winch serves all five lines, held in place by jammers.

severe weather conditions no more than an appropriate effort by the crew will bo noodod to oporato it.

Weak points can usually be recognised in good time; here are some typical parts which can cause problems and need watching continuously:

Halyards are particularly heavily stressed where they are led around halyard sheaves; individual wires projecting from the strands are the first signs of wear. Sharp-edged crimping sleeves can also do damage; here again the breaking of fine individual wires can be recognised in good time.

Shackles whose bolts have become bent must be exchanged for others better able to take the load. Swivel-shackles which are subject to particularly high dynamic loading should be tightened using pliers. Additional wrapping with tape does increase security but may conceal a bent bolt.

Cam-cleats may be expensive, but when buying them take care to choose proven brands. When sailing in salt water, salt crystals accumulate inside the clamps, so they should be cleaned out thoroughly with fresh water after every cruise.

An arrangement for turning the hauling parts of a main boom kicking strap which involves high friction losses. Separate guide-pulleys would be better.

Blocks — as for cam-cleats above.

Traveller systems comprise rails and sliders. The rails are mostly made of aluminium alloy, but the slider-bearing surfaces are frequently of stainless hard metal — result, when heavily loaded they are pressed into the soft rail and leave score-marks. Once that has happened it is not long before the slider can only be moved along the rail with difficulty. It is, of course, possible to remove these score-marks with emery-cloth, but it is better to use runners with plastic ball-bearings.

Winches have innards that should receive attention once or twice during the season. Clearing out with paraffin and subsequent greasing with non-hardening grease is all that is needed. Spares held on board should include pawls and the associated springs.

Mast and boom fittings are mostly fastened with blind rivets. Due to alternating loading these may slack off and eventually shear; slackening can also occur due to corrosion. Careful inspection allows such defects to be recognised in time.

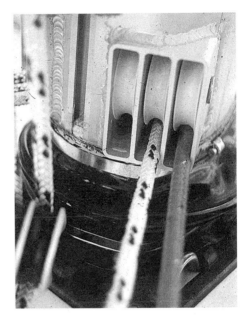

Boatyard sin: the halyards chafe against the sharp edge of the sheave-slot in the mast and will soon be ruined.

Spreader mountings may become excessively stressed, especially where the mast rake is variable; cracks in the mountings may result.

Rigging screws themselves scarcely ever break; problems are usually caused by missing split pins, or insufficiently tightened locknuts. A precaution that has proved most effective is to wrap tape around the screws.

Gooseneck fittings become heavily stressed, particularly if you are doing a lot of running free. Aluminium fittings get thinner and weaker with time, and eventually break.

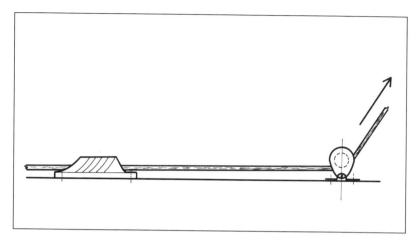

A practical belaying device. The right hand end of the hauling part is taken through a block. A pull to the right from beyond the block, and the line automatically belays in the clam cleat.

Trimming Controls for the Mainsail

Main Halyard

It is basically true to say that a mainsail is only drawing at its best when it has no creases. The only exceptions occur with some racing-class boats under extreme wind conditions (more about that in the chapter on dinghy rigs). If the halyard is set up too tight, a clearly visible parallel crease will appear near the luff. The consequence is that the belly of the sail is trimmed too far forward and the luff area of the sail is flattened too much.

If, however, the halyard is not set up tight enough several creases will slant across the sail, starting from the clew and radiating towards the luff. These airflow-disrupting creases become particularly visible if the luff has sliders holding it to the mast; the creases then end at these.

The principal cause of the luff sagging is stretch in the halyard. The more the halyard stretches in strengthening wind the more the luff will sag. The consequence is that the mainsail bellies more, the leech automatically closes more. The boat starts to carry weather helm; its close-hauled performance deteriorates.

The fatal element of a main halyard with too much stretch is that it operates in direct opposition to the proper trim of the sail. In light winds you normally want a more strongly bellying mainsail,

Even so-called 'pre-stretched' rope halyards begin to stretch as the wind strengthens. Result: the mainsail luff sags. Remedy: fit a wire halyard (with a rope tail).

but the halyard tends to shrink when lightly loaded, consequently tightens the luff and thus achieves a flatter sail profile. Inversely in a fresh wind, the halyard stretches and thus slackens the luff — the mainsail then bellies. Which halyard material to choose? Whereas the information about rope-breaking loads can be found in almost every yacht chandler's catalogue, there is a shortage of specific statements, not to mention figures, as regards stretching behaviour. Promotional statements such as 'very little stretch', 'pre-stretched' or 'limited extendibility' are little help when you are trying to decide what to buy. In practice a halyard should only be stressed to about 40 per cent of its breaking load. The way ropes stretch varies with load ranges, so if a percentage stretch is given, that relates to a predetermined range; the stress-strain curves are thus not linear.

If the stretch of 'pre-stretched' and 'not pre-stretched' halyard material is compared, it is noticeable that there are only small differences. In both cases the stretch in comparable load ranges is such that halyard tension has to be adjusted for varying wind strengths.

The stress-strain curve for a Kevlar® halyard shows clearly that this fibre's stretch is only about one-fifth that of standard rope, but still greater than that of wire. A halyard of that material would need only slight adjustment for normal changes in wind strength; at most some small tension adjustment might be needed for delicate racing trim. In view of the high purchase price, Kevlar® cordage will have difficulty in establishing itself against steel wire among the cruising and occasionally-racing fraternity. Kevlar® may only weigh half as much as steel, but the preference of cruising yachtsmen for high-CG roller headsail reefing gear proves that the small share of the total weight which the halyard constitutes is scarcely of any significance for cruising craft.

The stress-strain curves of galvanised and stainless wire are similar; the maximum stretch is minimal in both cases, so that the height of the mainsail head remains substantially unchanged regardless of changes in wind strength. Halyard tension adjustment is scarcely necessary, even under racing conditions or with the wind strength varying considerably. When choosing a halyard material, account must be taken of what one intends to do with the boat and what quality is appropriate to the state of the sails. For comfortable puttering around without any desire to sail fast, the cheapest will do. However, anyone conscious of the interplay between halyard stretch and sail trim will choose either wire or, if he wants to save weight, Kevlar®. Wire has the advantage of high mechanical loadability as regards friction. The only question remaining is: galvanised or stainless?

Sailors who race normally stress their rig much more heavily than is the habit among those who cruise. The consequence is that the wear and tear on the halyards is particularly high around the halyard sheaves and where they are belayed. That usually leads to a weakening of the halyard due to individual thin wires detaching themselves from the strands. Everyone is aware of these danger-ous 'meathooks'. The halyard must then be replaced by a new one, often before the end of even a single sailing season. If using stain-less wire, that can be expensive. An unnecessary expense, so why not use galvanised? It is not corrosion that is making replacement necessary, but the high mechanical stress.

Cruising produces a different set of conditions. The halyards

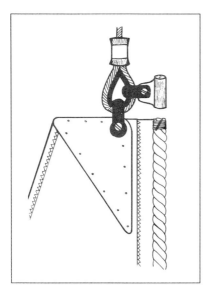

A slide above the mainsail head reduces the horizontal pulling forces on the end of the luff. There is less strain on the top edge of the sail between headboard and bolt rope and it should therefore last longer.

are less heavily stressed and remain in use for many, many years. In this case and taking the long-term view, non-corroding wire is better value for money. By the way, if you want to take care of your wire cordage, see to it that the sheave diameter is not less than ten times that of the wire. Bigger is always better. If you do not take that into account the thin individual wires in the strands can be stretched excessively by kinking. They break, and the wire is weakened.

Main Boom Kicking Strap

The kicking strap is one of the most important pieces of trimming equipment on board, particularly when reaching or running. Its tasks are as follows:

1.   To prevent the main boom lifting when reaching or running. This avoids excessive twisting of the sail; the leech remains closed. When running before a gale, there is additionally a safety aspect — if the mainsail is twisted too far, windward forces are generated in

the masthead region. The boat begins to sheer uncontrollably, alternately to windward and to leeward, a motion called yawing.

2. To control the twist of the leech when reaching. If the kicking strap is set up too hard, the leech closes too much; the airflow leaving the sail no longer does so smoothly, but instead breaks off at the leech, creating turbulence. Tell-tales along the leech show this clearly by blowing forward on the leeward side of the sail. If the kicking strap is not set up hard enough, the sail begins to spill the wind near the top of the leech sooner than it should; driving force is lost.

3. To influence the mast bend near the foot. This particularly applies to dinghy rigs. Namely, if the kicking strap is set up hard it pulls the boom forward. This in turn pushes the mast forward so that it develops curvature. The mainsail lower portion flattens.

Since the kicking strap is so important the crew on dinghies and small yachts must be able to adjust it from both sides of the craft.

If your choice of kicking strap is not affected by any ambition to race, you will be adequately served by a simple two- or three-part tackle. But if you also want to be able to work it while sailing, you have to choose a version which can be manipulated with a normal amount of force even in rough weather. For any type of strap, the material used must be adequately dimensioned, because the forces that arise can be very substantial. To minimise the stretch of a kicking strap, a wire strop should be used.

In physical terms, kicking-strap tackles constitute a purchase comprising standing and moving blocks. Fixed blocks are those that remain in place when the hauling part is worked; moving blocks, those that change position when the tackle is used. By using a fixed block, no reduction in the force required can be achieved, merely a change in its direction; by using a moving block, the magnitude of the force can be affected.

Tackles can be individually fashioned and are pretty failure-proof. But watch out for blocks that are too small; they may cause chafing of the ropes. An interesting variant of the kicking-strap tackle is the 'dory tackle' (Spanish loading tackle) — see illustration p. 23 — familiar from Spain and modified somewhat. In spite of having six parts, this tackle makes do with only three moving blocks; normally six sheaves would be needed. This means less

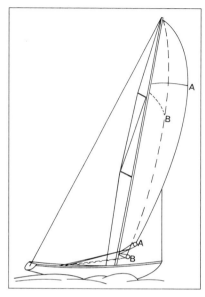 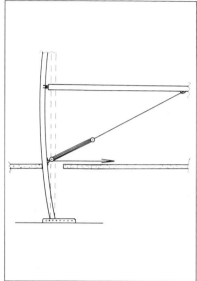

Position A: In the absence of a main boom kicking strap the sail twists.

Position B: A strap set up hard closes the leech and sees to it that the whole surface of the sail contributes to the propulsive power.

A kicking strap set up hard not only pulls the boom downwards but also forwards against the mast. If that has enough clearance in the deck opening, it bends.

friction, and furthermore it is very cheap.

Kicking straps with levers are particularly effective since only minimal frictional resistance has to be overcome. Disadvantage: they need more room than tackles. Many levers have the lever-effect (force amplification) adjustable by allowing the wire from the boom to be shackled to the lever in a number of different places. In this way, the lever can be matched specifically to the power available on board. The upper end of the lever should be pulled towards the gooseneck by means of an elastic cord to prevent the lever tipping over.

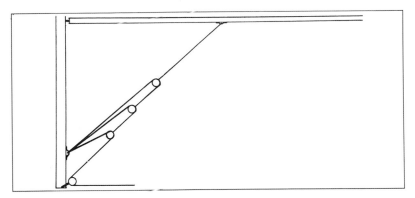

An interesting variant of the main boom kicking strap is the Spanish 'Dory tackle'. Only three moving blocks are needed to give the power advantage.

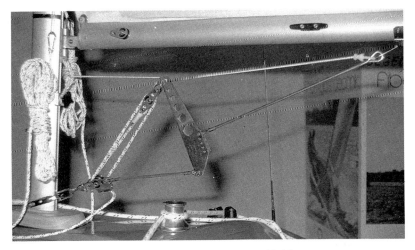

Lever tensioners are particularly suitable for kicking straps on dinghies and smaller yachts. The lever advantage can be individually adjusted by means of the five small holes. The harder the rope tackle is set up, the tauter the two wires are hauled. The elastic cord is to prevent the lever's top-end tipping over.

A tubular kicking strap with coarse and fine adjustment. Coarse adjustment is achieved by moving the slider underneath the boom horizontally; fine, by means of the wire tackle paralleling the tube.

Another possible means of tensioning a kicking strap is a drum with differing diameters along its length. The load part is wound around a small-diameter steel shaft, the hauling part around a larger-diameter plastic drum.

'Muscle boxes' can be fitted simply and without taking up a lot of space. If the hauling part can change direction, fitting in less accessible places (on board dinghies) is also possible. Disadvantages of muscle boxes: they are rather expensive, more expensive at any rate than comparable bare tackles with the same performance. Also they increase friction.

A tubular kicking strap offers the advantage that even without a topping lift, the boom cannot drop down onto the deck. This version only allows coarse adjustment and when sailing can only be worked with difficulty.

A preventer (arrowed) pulls the free end of the main boom forward and in heavy seas prevents an accidental gybe. If a gybe nevertheless occurs in a strong wind, this auxiliary line must be cast off at once, otherwise there is a danger of the yacht broaching-to with the mainsail aback and possibly being swamped.

BOONE COUNTY

1145426

Luff Tensioner (Cunningham)

Setting up the main halyard in a fresh wind requires great effort, as the frictional resistance of the halyard sheave and the halyard fairlead blocks has to be overcome. A means of tensioning the luff that requires less effort is a luff tensioner. This involves an eyelet pressed into the sail a few centimetres above the track, via which the sail is pulled downwards tensioning the luff. To do the pulling either a tackle is used — normal for dinghies and small yachts — or, on larger yachts, a winch. An English sailor called Cunningham introduced this method of luff-tensioning into yachting. Predominantly these tensioners are fitted to mainsails, but they may also be found fitted to headsails.

Apart from serving the purpose of trimming the for'd part of a mainsail flat and at the same time displacing the belly of the sail forward, a luff-tensioner set up hard also opens out the leech. A welcome trimming effect in strengthening wind that reduces the tendency to carry weather helm.

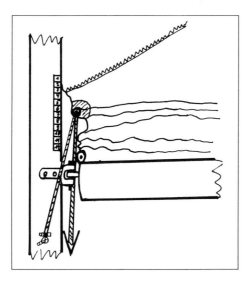

A Cunningham flattens the luff region of the mainsail and simultaneously opens the leech.

The length of a mainsail luff should be such that when the halyard is set up, the head exactly reaches the black band around the masthead. Where there is no measurement restriction, the head may be hauled up to just below the halyard sheave. In both cases this should leave the luff not yet set up hard; rather its tension should correspond to a sail profile as for light winds. If the wind strengthens, progressive hardening-up of the luff tensioner will keep the luff tension right. The end of travel for the Cunningham is just above the main boom. By the time it gets there, the for'd part of the sail must be trimmed as flat as possible. With the tensioner slacked-back, the distance of the eyelet from the boom must be chosen by the sailmaker so that the entire range of trim settings can be achieved.

Many mainsails can be observed to have a luff that is too short. The consequence is that when the halyard is set up, the luff region looks like a board; the tension is too great. So the halyard has to be eased again if the profile has to be deliberately deepened for very light winds. Sail area is being given away.

If such a sail does not have a Cunningham, luff tension must be corrected by means of the halyard. However, we know that in stormy winds this requires a lot of effort, and that setting up the halyard stresses the masthead-sheave heavily — particularly when sailing close to the wind. In that situation, the main sheet and kicking strap should be eased briefly to take the pressure off the sail and thus also off the halyard. Now the mainsail halyard can be set up tight without too much effort; in the case of small yachts it does not even call for a winch. After setting up the halyard the sheet is hauled taut again. With a practised crew, a bare five seconds will suffice for this evolution.

In conclusion let me point out a trim peculiarity. As far as luff tension is concerned, it makes no difference whether it is achieved by using a luff tensioner or by setting up the halyard tighter. However, unless the main sheet is adjusted there is a differing reaction from the leech: when the tensioner is used it opens; setting up the halyard tighter closes it.

Clew Outhaul

The effect on the overall sail camber of altering the foot tension is far less complex than that of altering the luff tension. Only the bottom part of the sail is affected by the clew outhaul. If the foot is hauled taut, all that happens is that the lower part of the sail goes flat; ease it as far as possible and you get the maximum possible camber depth.

The length of a mainsail foot is usually such that when the clew is hauled out to the black band on the guide roller the belly is trimmed flat. If you ease the outhaul, the clew slides forward along the boom until the amount of camber is a maximum. Such a sail is giving away surface area (unless class rules prohibit a flattening reef) because the available area is not being used to the full.

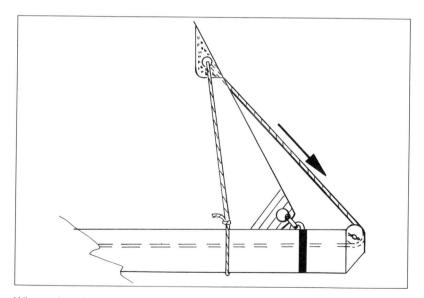

Where the clew of a mainsail has reached the 'black band' around the boom end, but the sail foot is still too slack, the camber can be flattened by means of a flattening reef.

For a flattening reef, an eyelet is pressed into the mainsail leech a few centimetres above the clew. This eyelet is pulled at an angle downwards and aft by means of a line, so that it can be used to trim the lower part of the sail flat. If a flattening reef is provided for, the mainsail foot length can be designed so that in a light wind the clew is hauled out to the black band, the sail then being set to belly. As the wind strengthens, the increasingly tensioned flattening reef sees to it that the camber depth of the lower part is set correctly. In principle the effect is similar to that of the Cunningham tensioner on the luff. The end of travel for the flattening-reef eyelet is just above the main boom. When it gets there the lower part of the sail must be trimmed as flat as it can be. Where a flattening reef is used, the foot can thus be made the maximum length — and that increases the sail area. There is thus no clew outhaul in the conventional sense; the clew is belayed firmly. In small boats the flattening reef can be worked by means of a tackle, which for instance can be run inside the boom. On larger yachts it makes sense to use a winch.

If the panel forming the foot of a mainsail is made of soft cloth, trimming the sail by means of the flattening reef is particularly easy and effective.

Influencing the camber depth by means of a clew outhaul or flattening reef is particularly effective if the bottom panel of cloth of the mainsail has a concave or bag-like shape and is unresinated. Such cloth is soft, flexible and easier to trim. This should be borne in mind when next ordering a mainsail.

Reefing

As you will be reading later, a deep sail camber can be expedient even in a fresh wind when beating, if the wave pattern is particularly disturbed. If it should be necessary to reef, the leads of the reefing pendant for the first reef must be positioned correctly. If they are too far aft, the pendant will pull the sail too far aft at the level of the reef points. The consequence is that the lower part of the mainsail is as stiff as a board. If you are aiming for a bellying profile, the reefing pendant leads must be moved further forward, so adjustable leads are useful. When taking down the second reef, on the other hand, some flattening of the camber is usually appropriate, so that the leads of that pendant may be located further aft on the main boom.

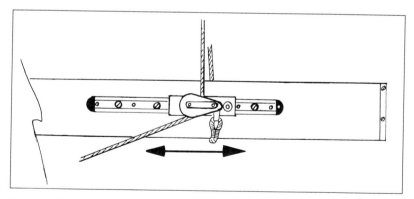

The reefing pendant leads should be movable along the main boom to allow foot tension to be varied – particularly in the case of the first reef.

The purpose of the reefing eyelets (holes punched in a horizontal line through the sail) is purely to lash the sailcloth loosely, not to trim the camber. For that reason racing yachts often do not have them. In this case make sure that the wind cannot blow from ahead into the reefed part of the sail hanging down loosely from the boom, which would slow you down. To avoid this, that part should be tied up somewhere near the for'd end, behind the gooseneck.

Main Sheet and Leech

The tail spoiler of a fast car and the leech of a mainsail have the same task: they are intended to ensure that the airflow leaving the object (car, mainsail) is smooth; any swirling of the flow is to be avoided. All turbulent flow increases the drag and that has a braking effect. Something similar is known from dinghy sailing: if the transom is pressed down into the water too far because the crew is sitting too far aft, the stern begins to 'suck'. The onward flow of water from the stern is disrupted, eddies are formed, and they slow the boat down. A similar effect is known, also from sailing: if the boat is carrying a lot of weather helm and you pull the tiller too hard, eddies form at the rudder blade. The rudder suddenly loses effect. In this case the water flow-pattern has broken down and the turbulence generated has a braking effect.

For as long as a boat can be sailed to windward upright, in accordance with its design lines, the main sheet may be hauled very taut and the leech closed. This way, the mainsail provides maximum energy and therefore driving force. If the wind gets stronger, the closed leech increases the heeling effect — and too much heel has a braking effect. Even modern keel-yachts with a flat bottom can put up with only about 15 to 20 degrees of heel; beyond that they slow down progressively. Yachts with the traditional rounded lines under water can stand a bit more; they reach their limit roughly when the water laps over the lee deck edge.

If the heeling limit is exceeded you should first open the leech to reduce the wind pressure on the upper and after part of the mainsail. That is achieved by either easing the main sheet, moving the traveller slider to leeward, or increasing the mast bend. Open-

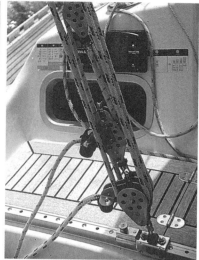

Mainsheet with two hauling parts. If you haul on both, the sheet moves rapidly but a great deal of effort is needed; if on just one, you get only half the speed of movement but it also needs only half the effort. The angle of the cam cleats can be varied by means of the four holes in the pivoted support-backets.

The first part of the sheet has an additional tackle shackled on. This allows the pull of the sheet to be adjusted easily and delicately once it has been hauled in to roughly the right extend with the main hauling part.

ing the leech allows the wind more freedom to flow away from the sail; the heel is reduced. The boat sails better. If the pressure near the leech becomes excessive the boat will try to climb to windward; this may get so bad that the helmsman even loses control of the boat and it 'shoots up into the wind'. A dangerous situation if there are other boats close-by to windward and the danger of a collision arises.

The mainsail leech should be adjusted to harmonise with the airflow over the sail, particularly in light airs if there is a bit of a sea running. The leech must be able to 'breathe' — you must not sail with it rigid, i.e. with the sheet too taut. The motion of the boat must be harmonised with the twist of the sail towards the head. If the sail has too little twist, the airflow is breaking away from the leech. This effect increases with mast height, since the magnitude of the movement due to the roll increases towards the masthead.

As a rule, if the wind is light and the sea smooth, you need only a little twist; you can haul the mainsheet in taut, depending on the strength of the wind. If the wind is light and there is a sea running, the leech has to be opened a little more, initially by easing the sheet. The effect of setting the leech properly can be demonstrated nicely by using tell-tales (more about that in the section on mainsail tell-tales).

Leech Line

Most mainsails have a thin line running inside the leech seam. The purpose of this line is to prevent the leech fluttering between the battens, so only tighten it enough to prevent flutter. If you pull it too taut it will prevent shaking, but the leech then gets a 'hook' in it. This pulls the leech to windward and that has the same effect as landing-flaps on an aircraft — braking.

However, there is one exceptional situation where this line can suitably be used to set the camber depth: in light to medium strength winds, when sailing with the wind from dead astern. First of all the kicking strap is eased slightly, then the line is hauled taut. Result: the leech closes noticeably, deepening the camber of the mainsail beyond the normal. The resistance coefficient increases; the sail draws better. But remember — when you next turn towards the wind, slacken the line again.

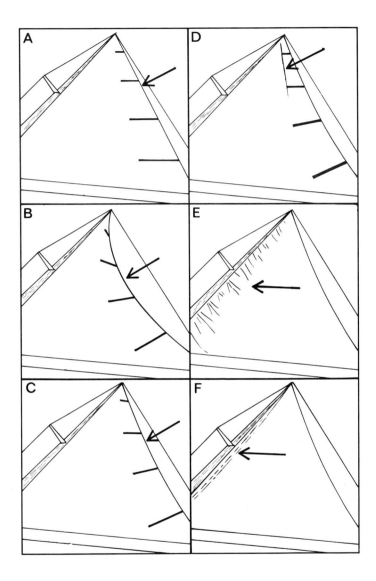

Mainsail trim (Figure opposite)
A: Mainsheet or kicking strap too taut. Leech too closed.
B: Mainsheet or kicking strap too slack. Leech too open.
C: Open leech correctly positioned.
D: For'd part top battens not flexible enough. A typical fold forms just
   for'd of them.
E: Luff not taut enough. Typical folds form in leading edge of sail.
F: Luff too taut. Typical folds form parallel mast.

Leech lines should be shortened
as much as possible to prevent
their becoming hooked into
something and possibly tearing
the leech.

Sail Battens

Sail battens must be light, yet strong enough not to break in strong winds or if the sail shakes. Furthermore, they must be flexible enough to harmonise with the sail camber. Reconciling these criteria poses no problem in the case of the lower battens (usually three in number); problems do, however, arise frequently with the top batten. On the one hand the for'd portion must be flexible enough to avoid a kink forming in the camber at the batten pocket's for'd end. On the other, the after section must be stiff enough to withstand high loading when the leech is shaking — so individual top battens are subject to differing requirements which can only be met by a varying flexural characteristic. Often, top battens are too stiff, so that you get a typical perpendicular fold near the pocket in the upper part of the sail. When the top batten extends right across the sail, that problem essentially cannot occur because the pocket ends at the sail luff. Always remember that the thick part of a batten should be nearest the leech.

To get a mainsail setting properly, a full-width batten is always worthwhile; it is all the more difficult to understand why so many one-design classes not constrained by formulae do not exploit this.

Tell-tales Along the Leech

Tell-tales on the mainsail and headsails indicate the aerodynamic conditions (i.e. the pattern of the airflow over the sails) very accurately. Indicators of this type are, for instance, also used in wind tunnels when carrying out fluidic investigations on objects. They reveal turbulence, including that generated by a badly set leech. Admittedly a cockpit full of electronic wind indicators looks very smart and may leave third parties much impressed, but tell-tales tell you more about the correct trim of the sail. Furthermore they are cheap and easy to fix. Even Admiral's Cup yachts cannot do without them.

Mainsail tell-tales are fastened to the leech. Four strips of spinnaker cloth, each about 20 cm. long, are the norm, positioned near the batten pockets. Woollen tell-tales are no good because the

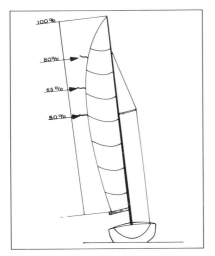

Suggested positions for tell-tales of spinnaker cloth, along the leech of a mainsail.

shaking of the leech in strong winds soon makes them fray, and they also tend to stick to the sail when wet.

If the angle of incidence and the twist of the mainsail relative to the wind is correct, the flow over the sail will be laminar and undisturbed; there will be no significant braking zones of turbulent flow. The leech tell-tales indicate this by flying horizontally aft. But if this angle is enlarged, either by hauling the sheet in too far or by letting the boat's head fall off, the flow over the leeward face of the sail separates, beginning at the leech and progressing for'd as the setting deteriorates further. A turbulent 'wake' develops to leeward of the sail. Turbulent airflow endeavours to maintain the overall circulation around the sail; some flow is set up which opposes the direction in which the boat is sailing. The leech tell-tales respond promptly: those on the leeward side of the sail disappear suddenly and fly forward, lying close to the sail as they do so. Either the sail has to be eased or the boat brought closer to the wind.

In practice it is not difficult to get the lower two strips to fly horizontally aft, but the top one always tries to hide to leeward of the sail. It calls for considerable skill and attention on the part of the helmsman to get this top strip to fly properly. There will always be the need to balance between a disappearing top tell-tale and backwinding in the mainsail's luff region.

If the sheet is too slack and the sail's angle of incidence relative to the wind becomes too acute, it will cause the luff to backwind violently.

Tell-tales also have a psychological effect. Imagine racing without tell-tales; the crew sits high up on the side deck to trim the boat as upright as possible. The helmsman concentrates his attention on the electronic instruments in the cockpit, visible only to him. Only he can identify his mistakes, the crew cannot observe them. (The best preconditions for sailing the boat backwards!) With tell-tales, on the other hand, his slack steering is clearly visible to the crew. And since sitting along the toe-rail trimming the boat is normally a tedious business, the crew likes to look for some variety — for instance by watching the tell-tales. This provides a check on the helmsman, and often after the crew has told him for the n-th time 'to steer a bit more carefully', he may hand over the tiller to someone more skilled or less tired.

To sum up: tell-tales are honest indicators of the correct trim of a sail. They can be observed by the crew, and for that reason alone are justifiable trimming aids.

The Topping Lift

This is intended to prevent the main boom dropping onto the deck or becoming trapped in the guardrails during the reefing process, or to support the boom when the mainsail is lowered. It has nothing to do with the trim of the mainsail, but remember that if it is set up too taut it may adversely affect the leech tension. The effect would be to open the leech permanently, preventing the sail from 'breathing'. The air would flow weakly past the leech without exerting any pressure on the sail. The lift must always be eased sufficiently to prevent it becoming tensioned even with the sheet hauled in hard. Sometimes, however, in very light conditions it may be used to support the boom and encourage the sail to assume a fuller shape.

The Traveller

The traveller assembly comprises a rail and a runner; its purpose is to control the twist of the mainsail. When mounting a traveller on a boat, care must be taken to see that the main sheet/boom connection is vertically above it when the boom is centred. If the wind varies greatly in strength, it will be necessary to move the traveller when beating. Its operating lines must therefore be easy to reach from either side of the cockpit and operable by the crew with no more than normal effort.

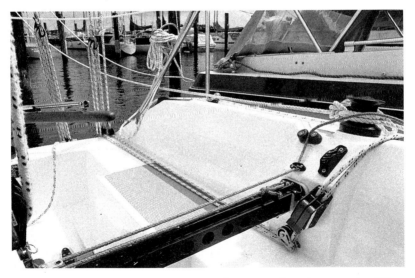

The traveller line can be reached easily even when the crew is sitting on the sidedeck. For'd of the traveller rail is the running backstay for coarse and fine adjustment. The clam cleat below the winch is for the spinnaker sheet. Standing backstay adjustments are made directly at the transom.

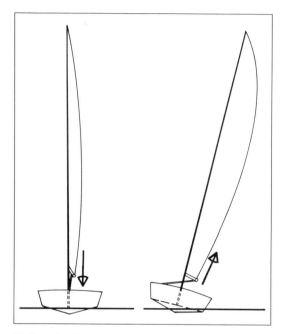

Mainsail trim for light airs:
LH – the mainsheet led from the centreline pulls the boom down; the leech is too closed.
RH – the sheet led from the windward side plus the heel of the boat give the leech the correct amount of twist.

In light winds the traveller may be utilised to open the mainsail leech somewhat: with the mainsheet-pull vertical the leech is pulled downwards and closes fully, even in light winds when the sheet is fairly slack. This effect is augmented by the weight of the boom. The leech now sets in a straight line. If a light gust arises, this straight line will be the cause of turbulent flow at the leech; the tell-tales along it fold to leeward behind the sail. The leech must be opened; in light gusts it must be able to breathe, to adjust to harmonise with the airflow. Only if the flow past the leech is laminar will the sail function efficiently.

This breathing is made possible by having the mainsheet-pull slanting to windward. The boom must not be pulled to windward beyond the centreline, so for this experiment the sheet must be eased as necessary. If the sheet pulls not vertically but at a slant, then in a light gust the boom can lift more easily to open the leech. The flow over the sail is improved; it draws. If the wind strengthens somewhat, this exercise of having the sheet pulling from the windward side is abandoned to prevent excessive floating of the leech. The traveller can be brought back to amidships, and can stay there until the boat's heel becomes excessive. If wind-strength then continues to increase, the traveller has to be let down to leeward; that takes some of the wind pressure off the leech, easing the load on the rudder and hence weather helm.

The traveller's effectiveness reduces when, running before the wind, the main sheet has been eased so far that the boom is no longer over the traveller rail. Control of the mainsail twist is then exercised predominantly via the kicking strap.

Trimming Controls for the Headsail

Headsail Halyard

As far as materials are concerned, the arguments which apply to the mainsail halyard apply also to that for the headsail. In the headsail, too, characteristic folds appear if the luff tension is not right. With the luff insufficiently taut, the typical folds run from luff to clew; furthermore the leech is closed. A luff hauled too tight shows itself by a fold parallel to the forestay running from the head of the sail to the tack. To avoid either, the halyard tension must always be adjusted to the wind strength. Rule of thumb: high wind — high tension; light breezes — lower tension.

Forestay

Forestay tension plays a significant part in determining close-hauled sailing performance: the less the forestay sags to leeward, the closer to the wind you can sail. A tight forestay produces flatter camber with less belly, and therefore a more favourable pointing ability. It follows, therefore, that the more the forestay sags to

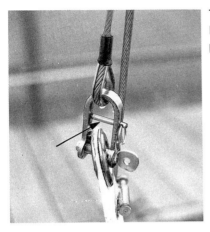

This kind of shackle stops you losing either the main body or the pin.

Typical luff-region fold formation; the halyard has not been set up tight enough.

leeward, the more the headsail bellies. The leech closes, and where there is a Genoa with an extensive overlap on the mainsail this will cause weather helm.

When manufacturing a headsail, the sailmaker must know how much the forestay sags to leeward when sailing. This is easy enough to establish: in a wind of strength appropriate to the sail, you sail as close to the wind as possible — the stay will sag to leeward under the pressure from the sail. To determine the extent

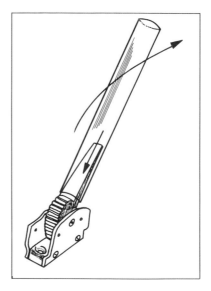

If a jammer with load on it cannot be opened because the lever is too short, a metal tube slid over the arm increases the leverage. This seldom fails to work.

With the aid of a muscle box, the headsail halyard can be set up really hard. They are available in various lengths and with varied gearing.

Plastic tubes do not only protect the rigging screws, they also ensure that the hanks cannot slide beyond the forestay and fitting and thus risk getting skewed when the sail is hoisted.

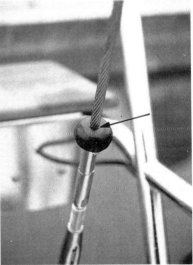

A ball will prevent the hanks sliding down onto the end fitting.

of this sag, you hook a second halyard into the forestay deck fixture and set this up very taut; it now lies roughly in a straight line. By measuring the maximum distance between forestay and halyard (the chord of the arc), the maximum sag to leeward can be established fairly accurately. The sailmaker will take that measurement into account when cutting the luff to shape and thus can embody the right amount of camber.

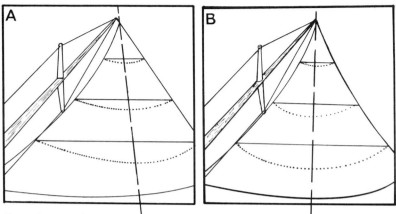

Forestay tension

A: The forestay is set up hard. The headsail camber reaches a maximum at about one-third width from the luff. The sail is trimmed flat. The boat will point as well as is possible.

B: The forestay sags to leeward. The camber increases and its maximum depth moves aft, to about the middle of the sail. A profile that produces a lot of power, but the boat will not point well.

Sheet Leads

Setting the leads in the right place is one of the most difficult, and at the same time most important, trimming operations. The leads' position depends on:

- the strength of the wind
- the wind incidence-angle
- the sea state
- the mast rake.

An accurate impression of whether headsail sheet leads are in the right or the wrong place is best obtained by looking at the sail from astern and to leeward. Better still, get into another boat and sail

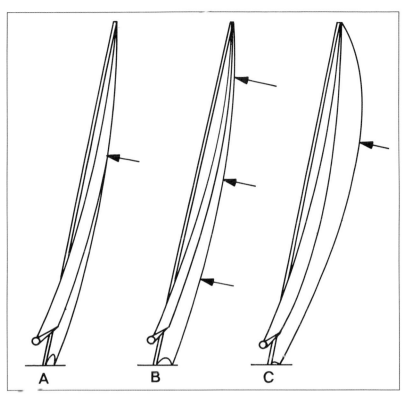

Headsail sheet lead settings
A: The lead is set too far for'd, the leech is too closed.
B: Head and mainsail profiles harmonise, the lead is in the right
   place.
C: The lead is set too far aft, the leech is too open.

astern and to leeward of the headsail to be adjusted. Every skipper should seize the opportunity to assess the trim of his sails from 'outside' — it is a worthwhile exercise.

As a first rough approximation, the lead should be set so that sail foot and leech tension are about the same — when on a beat. Furthermore, the after portion of the headsail should set roughly parallel to the upper shrouds.

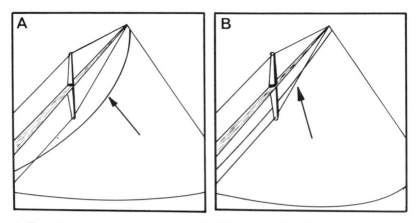

A: The sheet lead must be moved for'd to close the Genoa's leech more.

B: The sheet lead is set too far for'd. The leech is too closed.

A second, somewhat more accurate method consists of observing what the luff looks like just as it stops drawing. To this end you sail close-hauled, a bit too close to the wind. If the area that stops drawing extends evenly all along the luff (i.e. runs parallel with it) the lead is in the right place. If it is only in the upper part of the sail, the lead must be moved forward or downward — and vice versa. The ideal position has been reached when main and headsail harmonise, the headsail leech lying parallel to the mainsail profile. And the uniformity of the gap between the two sails is best judged from on board another boat. The positioning of the sheet lead depends on the strength of the wind. Assuming it is intended to trim the headsail to belly in light winds, the lead must then be moved forward somewhat. The first result of this is to close the leech too much, but checking the sheet a little will take that brake off again.

If the sheet lead is set correctly for light winds, it then has to be moved when the halyard is set up harder as the wind freshens. The leech becomes more closed, so the lead has to be pushed aft.

If the sailcloth stretches a lot under wind pressure, the leech opens automatically as the wind strengthens. There may then be no need to move the lead.

The Genoa sheet lead is in exactly the right place; mainsail and Genoa run parallel and harmonise.

Sheet lead positioning furthermore depends on the wind angle-of-attack. Sailing close-hauled it should be well inboard on the side deck. How far will depend on the type of boat. A rule-of-thumb for a modern cruising yacht is to place it by the cabin side-bulkhead; this lets you get close to the wind. When reaching, however, the lead needs to be outboard and forward. Easing the mainsheet reduces the gap between headsail leech and mainsail luff region. Backwinding appears near the mainsail luff. To open the slot again, the sheet lead must be moved outboard, right out to the deck edge. This lets the air flow away from the headsail more freely, the backwinding decreases, and the mainsail functions more effectively.

The sheet lead must additionally be moved for'd because as the foresheet is eased the headsail leech opens. Indeed, disproportionately more than the foot because it is longer. The result is well known: you are reaching, the lower part of the Genoa sets beauti-

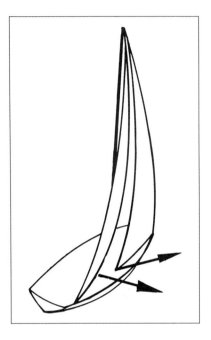

When reaching, the headsail sheet lead must be moved for'd and outboard.

fully but the upper part is spilling the wind. The leech has to be closed a bit, until the luff again stops drawing, uniformly and parallel to the forestay, if you sail too close to the wind. To achieve this, the sheet lead is moved for'd; by about a metre on a 9-metre keel boat.

If with the water relatively smooth the headsail is eased beyond its sheet lead, it must be set further for'd when the sea gets rougher — this is to deepen the sail camber. As is already known from the setting for light winds, the sheet must not be hauled so taut as to close the leech.

Photo right
Jib sheet lead adjustment on a '470'. The block can be pulled for'd on the rail by means of a line; the elastic cord should pull it aft again.

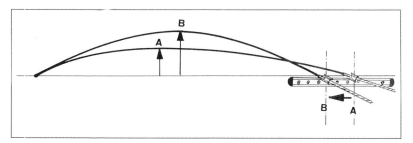

Moving the headsail sheet lead for'd (from A to B) makes the sail belly more. At the same time the sheet must be eased a bit to re-open the leech a little.

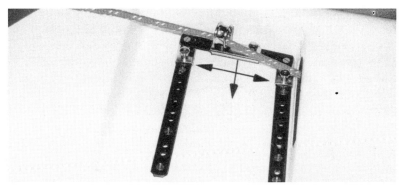

Genoa sheet lead adjustment that allows athwartship trim.

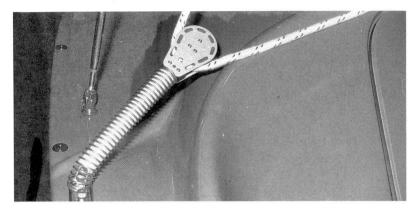

The headsail sheet track is mounted very far outboard on the sidedeck. If the block is set on it directly, the lead will be too far outboard: result – the boat will not point well. A strop between block and track brings the lead further inboard; the boat will point better. The steel spring sleeve visible in the photograph is intended to prevent the metal block damaging the plastic deck.

If the lead has been set for a given mast rake, it must be moved for'd if the rake is increased, because the distance between sail head and sheet lead is reduced, while the leech remains the same length. Were the lead left in its original position, the leech would open too much. Incidentally, this effect is used intentionally in modern racing dinghies to keep them sailing more upright in strong winds.

Sheet Leads for Roller-reefing Headsails

If you reduce the sail area of a roller-reefing headsail, the sheet lead must also be adjusted, particularly when close-hauled. Manufacturers of such equipment like to conceal this fact in order to emphasize their easy, simple, operation.

As you reef one of these headsails, the leech opens progressively. To close it again, you need to move the sheet lead for'd. Unless this is done, you will experience increasing weather helm with the decreasing sail area.

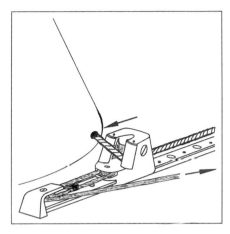

A headsail sheet lead slider whose position can be altered from the cockpit by means of a tackle. This adjustment also recommends itself if the headsail is a roller-reefing one, since there is no need to leave the protection of the cockpit.

Roller-reefing headsails are intended to reduce the discomfort of crewing a yacht. However if a defect develops at sea and in rough weather it can endanger the entire rig.

Moving the sheet-lead slider on the lee deck in heavy weather is not without its dangers, but there is a proven method for doing this from the safety of the cockpit. For this the slider must be able to move freely on the track. Its for'd end is connected to a tackle whose standing part is fixed to the for'd end of the track, and whose hauling part is taken to the cockpit. (see illustration top, page 53). Now if the lead has to be moved for'd because the headsail is half rolled up, all you do is haul on the tackle. To allow the slider to slide aft as the headsail area is increased, easing the tackle is quite sufficient; the pull of the sheet will bring it aft. Roller-reefing gear for headsails is justified for cruising because it is convenient. However, you do not see it on racing yachts because the setting of a partially rolled up Genoa is usually so baggy that the sailing characteristics close-hauled worsen drastically.

Sheet Leads for Self-tacking Jibs
Self-tacking jibs are primarily convenient in narrow waters and with a small family-crew, since they do not need to be worked when going about. The sheet can usually be shackled into one of several holes in a metal-reinforced broad clew, which alters the angle of pull of the sheet. Compared with the foot, self-tacking jibs have a very long leech, exceedingly sensitive to the sheeting angle: even an angle too steeply downwards will close the leech immediately — too horizontal an angle and it opens excessively. This supersensitive reaction of that kind of sail requires very careful trimming of the sheet lead.

Self-tacking jibs have the disadvantage that the sheet lead cannot be adjusted when running free. Once the traveller has reached the end of the track, all you can do when running free is ease the sheet. Normally the lead would need shifting for'd to avoid sailing with the leech too open. Changing the trim would necessitate moving the sheet shackle to a hole further up in the clew. As it is, you just have to accept that when running free the upper part of the jib will be open too wide — unless you just set the jib a bit higher, for example by fastening a tackle to the tack and easing this generously. At the same time you can harden-up on the halyard a bit more. This closes the leech more; the jib then draws better.

Sheet lead adjustment for a self-tacking jib. The sheet shackle can bc moved from one to another of the six holes in the metal clew plate.

Sheet guide of a self-tacking jib on a small racing yacht ('Fun'). The central traveller operating line is taken to the cockpit.

Barber Hauler

Barber haulers allow you to save time when adjusting headsail sheet leads. The sheet is rove through a block so that this comes between the headsail clew and the normal fairlead. By means of an extra line (with belaying facilities) led via a turning block, the sheet can be pulled out towards the turning block. This type of adjustment is useful for moving the lead between the close-hauled and running-free positions (see illustration p. 56).

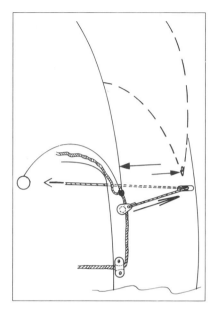

Barber hauler. For beating, the lead is inboard; the sheet is led via a turning block on the sidedeck. When reaching, the barber hauler is set up hard, moving the lead further for'd and outboard.

(Photo bottom left)
Lead adjustment by means of a barber hauler on an athwartship sheet rail. There is also another barber hauler for the spinnaker sheet lead. ('Sprinta Sport')

(Photo bottom right)
Barber hauler arrangement (arrowed) for moving the sheet leads on a small coastal cruiser (X 79).

Tell-tales

In the headsail, as is in the mainsail, tell-tales can be a very valuable trimming-aid. Woollen threads each about 30 cm. long are threaded through the sail with a sewing needle, about 20 cm. from the luff and spaced so as roughly to quarter its length. When locating them, care must be taken to prevent their getting too close to the sailmaker's zig-zag seams, because nothing is more irritating than the windward-side tell-tale standing vertical because the wool has caught in the seaming.

The woollen threads will soak up water — and so these splendid indicators malfunction when it is wet and there is little wind. Spraying them with a waterproofing substance keeps them going a bit longer, but causes the threads to lose their flexibility.

Lengths of cassette tape glued to the sail are very sensitive, but their fluttering is so unsteady that they cannot be recommended.

The airflow over the leeward side of a sail is more important than that over the windward side, because it determines the propulsive force. For that reason, the leeward threads need watching with special care. Dark threads make this easier because the dark colour shows up better through white sailcloth. Nevertheless, in particularly bright sunshine visibility on the windward side of the sail can get so bad than even a dark thread cannot be seen, so one should insist on having at least one small window in the headsail. If at its mid-height this circular window has a tell-tale on either side, both threads can easily be watched even under the most unfavourable conditions.

The threads function as follows: as long as the headsail has laminar flow on both sides, all six threads (three on the windward side and three on the leeward) will fly substantially horizontally aft. If the boat is sailed too close to the wind, the windward threads start to flutter, ultimately turning upwards. In light and medium-strength winds this change comes about very gradually and the helmsman can bear away at leisure.

The behaviour of the leeward threads, however, is distinctly hectic. If the helmsman bears away too far, these threads suddenly fly upwards or even for'd. The airflow over the leeward face of the sail has broken down; turbulent areas develop. It still looks to be

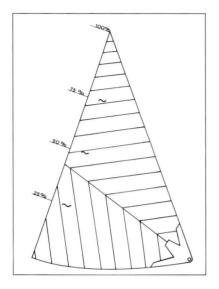

Suggested positions for tell-tales in the luff region of a Genoa.

set beautifully but it scarcely draws any longer. Now the helmsman must either luff up at once or the sheet must be eased.

The basic principle is therefore: the leeward tell-tales of a headsail when beating and when reaching must always fly horizontally aft, but not so the windward ones. The way they fly depends on the strength of the wind and the sea state. Whereas in a light wind they too should fly horizontally, they may as the wind strengthens turn upwards more. In a really strong wind that means about 70 degrees.

A rule-of-thumb is that with the best sailor's wind and not much sea running, the windward threads may fly upwards at about 30 degrees; that means the helmsman is sailing the boat close to the wind. With more of a sea running the boat needs more energy from the sail; the waves reduce the boat's way through the water more frequently, so that it has to accelerate again correspondingly frequently. That means increased wind pressure on the headsail, and the tell-tales are then not deflected upwards as much.

Tell-tales are also useful for getting the sheet-lead setting right. When correct all the tell-tales on both sides will be streaming the same way. That means that when pointing the boat too high or not

Heel of boat		
slight	medium	strong
WINDWARD		
LEEWARD		

As a boat heels more, so the tendency of the windward tell-tales to fly upwards may increase. The leeward tell-tales, however, should always fly horizontally aft.

The tell-tales in the Genoa on this 'Flying Dutchman' show that it is being sailed close-hauled and pointing as high as possible.

high enough, all three threads on one side will respond identically and in parallel. The upper pair reacts in the same way as the lower. However, if the lead is too far for'd, when luffing only the lower windward thread will flutter. The upper tell-tales will continue to signal 'all's well'. Only when luffing still further will the middle and finally the uppers indicate turbulence.

If on the other hand the sheet lead is too far aft, the upper part of the leech will open first. That means that for this part of the sail the wind angle-of-attack is too acute, so the upper windward tell-tale will flutter restlessly upwards, whereas the two lower ones continue to fly horizontally aft.

To use these excellent steering and trimming aids at night, most racing yachts have auxiliary spotlights installed. These are fitted below deck and shine through small windows in the foredeck or in the side decks. They are directed onto the most important set of tell-tales, usually the bottom pair. A pocket torch will do as well; the illumination must not be too strong, otherwise the white circle of light on the sail blinds the helmsman.

The Leech Line

Its purpose, as in the case of the mainsail, is not to trim the camber but merely to stop leech-flutter. Elderly headsails in particular tend to have a leech that is 'tired'; the leech line should only be hauled taut enough to stop the flutter. Leech lines with too much tail are especially dangerous; they can easily get caught up in the rig and tear the leech open from bottom to top. So: shorten to about 10 cm. if necessary.

The Sail Foot

When wind is blowing onto a sail, a depression forms on the lee-ward side. There is thus a pressure difference between the wind-ward and leeward sides of the sail; this generates the propulsive force. The less this pressure difference, the weaker the force generated.

Pressure equalisation between windward and leeward side will, for example, take place along the sail foot if it does not rest on the deck, so a No.1 Genoa should end at deck level. This of course has the disadvantage that the crew cannot see ahead, but that can be overcome by having a large window in the headsail. The transparent materials used for this purpose are very hard-wearing, but making sharp folds in them when folding the sails should be avoided.

Correct Camber

It is generally considered that in light winds a sail with deep camber draws better than one trimmed flat; a flat sail, on the other hand, is said to be right for strong winds.

In principle both views are correct — and yet situations frequently arise where a trim deviating from this principle is advantageous, because it is not only the strength of the wind that determines the choice of camber, but also the swell and boat's shape.

Let us assume you are beating with the sails trimmed flat in a fresh breeze and a smooth sea. The boat is sailing almost at hull speed:

$$\text{hull speed (knots)} = \sqrt{\text{waterline length (metres)}} \times 2.43$$

Some time later, you reach open water; there is an uncomfortable short sea running. The bow of the boat at intervals digs deep into the waves, slowing it down abruptly. After each almost total stop, it must accelerate again, calling for an extra amount of propulsive force to overcome the force of the waves. Thus the sails have to produce more power if there is a sea running than if the water is smooth.

So: the sails must, even when close-hauled, be set to a deeper

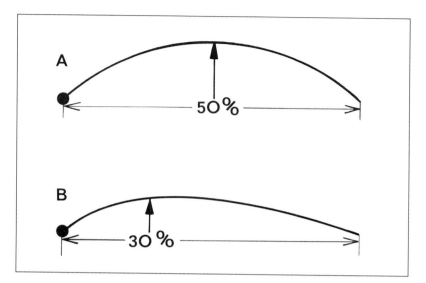

Where the sail camber is deep, the maximum depth is at about 50% of the sail width, ie midway between luff and leech. If the sail is trimmed flatter, the maximum depth moves for'd as the camber is reduced. You can get more power out of deep camber than out of shallow, but with the former the boat points less well.

camber because that provides more propulsive power, accepting at the same time that you cannot sail as close to the wind as previously.

An analogy may help to make this clear: cargo 'planes are intended for the transport of heavy goods, so their wing profile has to be such as to develop great lift. That calls for a high-energy, deep section. So, as observation on airfields will show, that type of aircraft has wings with an especially deep profile. Shallow profiles are used for fighter jets or gliders which do not need a high-energy profile, since their lift requirement is less than that of the cargo plane.

To demonstrate that even with little wind, trimming the sail flat can be advantageous, consider a different situation: an especially slender yacht, on a beat, can almost reach its hull speed with a wind no stronger than Force 3. The water is smooth and thus offers minimum resistance to the hull. Here, an early re-trim to flatten the sail profile is profitable, though there is only a 'gentle breeze'. If, however, the sails were set to belly — in accordance with the 'little wind = deep camber' principle — they could indeed provide more energy (propulsive power), but in this case the extra energy could only marginally be converted into extra speed since the yacht is already running almost at hull speed. The energy surplus would merely show up as additional pressure on the sail, which in turn would result in unnecessary, speed-reducing heel.

So if the water is smooth, sails may be trimmed flat earlier since wave resistance is absent. With a shallow camber you can sail closer to the wind than with a deep one.

Mast Rake

This means the inclination aft of the mast, so if the mast is vertical the rake is nil. The designation applies exclusively to the tilt of the mast, never to its bend.

Experience has shown that dinghies, catamarans, and even yachts have better sailing characteristics close-hauled in wind of medium or greater strength, particularly if there is a sea running, if the mast is raked. True, there are class-specific exceptions to this, for example in the case of the Soling. In this Olympic boat class, mast rake is used in light winds to get pressure on the mainsail leech, and thus on the rudder. As the wind increases, the mast is trimmed more upright to counter the weather helm which increases the heel.

A lot of rake means that the load comes off the bow of the boat, making it easier for the fore part to cut through the waves. This relief derives on the one hand from the transfer aft of the weight of the mast, on the other also from the reduced mass moment of inertia in the boat's longitudinal direction. Additionally with a mainsail set up tilted, the force produced is directed not only forwards but also upwards.

However, mast rake affects speed negatively when running

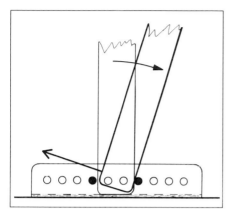

If the mast is raked particularly strongly, care must be taken to see that the heel is still sufficiently secure in the step. If not, it can easily spring out forwards.

before the wind. Then, the mainsail operates as a projected surface and this is reduced when the mast is tilted — so for running before the wind the mast has to be trimmed upright again. Sailing like this, the air flows onto the sail but scarcely around it; it acts merely as an obstruction to the wind, not as an aerodynamic profile. Flow past an obstruction generates turbulent flow on the downwind side; flow around a profile, on the other hand, a depression. Now, if you let the mast tip forward beyond the vertical, the flow is once again around the mainsail and a depression is generated to leeward; the boat speeds up. Such a mast trim — masthead tilted for'd — can be observed particularly on the Olympic 'stars'. This game with the mast rake can only be played with boats whose fixed shrouds are substantially abreast the mast. The mast foot can then act as a pivot and the mast tilts about this. The only rig suitable for this is $\frac{7}{8}$ (fractional) with running backstays. Dinghy rig calls for shroud adjusters that can be operated while sailing; primarily in the Flying Dutchman class.

   If the mast is to be brought upright for running, standing backstay and running backstays have to be slackened off; wind pressure in the sails will then automatically tilt the mast for'd. The

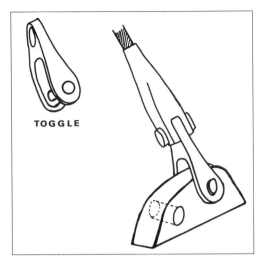

A toggle inserted between forestay and forestay chain-plate allows the mast rake to be increased.

forestay now hangs slack. Particularly with a sea running, the mast ought to be secured in that position, otherwise it will sway uncontrollably and could damage itself. Securing it is easy enough: either you harden down on the halyard of an already set headsail, or you shackle another halyard to the bow fitting and harden down on that.

Be careful. If in a strong blow the mast is to be brought to running-trim on completion of a close-hauled tack, the standing backstay must be slackened off first and only then the running backstay. If you slackened the runner first, the taut standing backstay would break off at the top of the mast backwards.

If a long-term increase of mast rake is planned for a yacht, various points need to be watched. First of all the forestay must be lengthened. For that, toggles (metal links for fitting between rigging screw and forestay chainplate) are available from the specialist trade. Possibly the standing backstay and the shrouds will also need adjusting. Then you must allow for the fact that increasing the mast rake brings the headsail clews further down. That applies particularly to the No.1 Genoa, whose foot is usually cut very low: if with the mast raked it is no longer possible to close the leech sufficiently, the sail must be altered. An alternative is to get the sailmaker to insert several sheet eyes, one above the other. With maximum rake, the sheet is then shackled to the top eye. Lastly you have to remember that the end of the main boom comes down; the limit of mast rake is reached when the boom only just clears the guardrail. More mast rake also means more weather helm, which may cause more problems than cures.

Weather Helm — Cause and Cures

Series-built yachts and dinghies are, as a rule, so constructed that if properly handled they are pretty well neutral on the helm. Indeed, a little weather helm should be welcome; lee helm is always undesirable. Excessive weather helm arises if the aggregate sail centre of effort lies aft of the underwater hull lateral pressure centre. This could be due to too much mast rake, or the sails bellying too much or being badly trimmed. Sometimes, however, it is the designer's fault or the builder's; if that is so then there is nothing for it but to make constructional changes such as:

- moving the keel surface aft
- extending the keel surface aft
- moving the mast for'd
- moving ballast further aft.

The last-named remedy can to a limited extent be applied by the owner himself; heavy pieces of equipment are stowed further aft, which brings the forebody up making it easier for the wind pressure on the headsail to push it to leeward. However, we want to concern ourselves with trimming steps the crew can take as regards the rig.

In most cases the responsibility for excessive weather helm rests with poor trim of the mainsail, particularly a leech that is too

If the mainsheet is over sheeted the wind pressure on the mainsail leech intensifies. Result: the boat acquires weather helm and heels alarmingly.

closed. That produces very high wind pressure on the battened part of the sail. The battens are aft of the boat's centre of rotation, so the after part is pushed to leeward, the bow to windward. Result: weather helm. To remedy this, the leech must be trimmed to open it more, by:

- setting up the main halyard hard
- setting up the luff tensioner hard
- setting up the foot outhaul hard
- easing the mainsheet slightly
- increasing the mast bend
- sliding the traveller to leeward
- taking in a reef, if she is heeling too much.

Another possible cause of weather helm is to oversheet the mainsail, with the foresheet lead outboard. To remedy this, the wind angle-of-attack must be about the same for head and mainsail; their surfaces should be substantially parallel. Either move the foresheet leads inboard or set the main boom further to leeward. If there is a traveller, it should be pushed to leeward; this leaves the sheet pulling vertically on the boom and avoids the sail twisting. If there is no traveller, the sheet must be eased. Simultaneous lifting of the main boom and thence twisting of the sail is avoided by setting up the kicking strap hard.

Here is a little trick for tightening even a simple, low-geared kicking strap without a lot of effort: turn the boat briefly into the wind and haul the mainsheet in fully, then set up the strap. When the sheet is then eased again, the strap is fully tensioned. If you lack a traveller, this method combined with easing the mainsheet is the only way excessive mainsail twist can be avoided.

Yet another possible cause of excessive weather helm is a Genoa bellying too much. Wind pressure on the leech then becomes so high that it sets up a luffing moment, because with the boat heeled the leech is aft of the centre of rotation. Remedies for flattening the Genoa and opening the leech are by:

- hardening down on the forestay
- hardening down on the Genoa halyard
- moving the sheet lead aft.

Lastly, in the case of modern yachts with a flat underwater hull, too much heel produces weather helm. It results in distortion, as it were, of the underwater-hull lines past which the water is flowing. This tendency can be demonstrated effectively in a boat with the tiller belayed amidships. If you make it heel by transferring weight to leeward, it takes on weather helm; if, on the other hand, you make it heel to windward it takes on lee helm. This sensitive reaction associated with modern hull shapes must be allowed for by sailing upright. That includes reefing in good time.

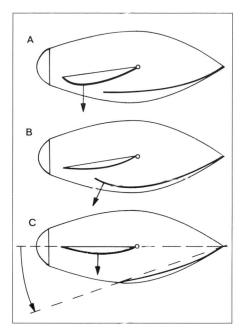

Three causes of weather helm

A: The mainsail is set too full and with the leech too closed. Wind pressure becomes very high towards the leech; a luffing-moment is established.

B: The Genoa is set too full and with the leech too closed; wind pressure on that region becomes very high. This is aft of the boat's turning point; the boat luffs up.

C: The headsail sheet lead is very far outboard on the sidedeck; at the same time the main boom is hauled in practically to the centreline by means of the mainsheet. A luffing-moment results.

Trim for Beating

Light Airs

If the wind strength is so low that the sails can barely assume their proper shape, trimming by shifting weight is effective since optimum propulsive power can only be obtained with the proper camber, not with the sail hanging down slackly. So you heel the boat to leeward, whereupon the weight of the cloth makes the sails set into their camber. They are now on 'standby' and able to start propelling at the slightest breath of wind. Leeward heel is achieved most effectively if you have crew not only at the widest part of the side deck, but also on the leeward side of the foredeck or even below decks. By trimming down-by-the-bow in this way the hull floats in a less stable attitude and is thus prepared to 'lean over' further. Furthermore, this trim reduces the wetted hull surface; that lowers the frictional resistance and adds a further gain in speed.

In light airs, any jerky movement by the crew leads to breakdown of the air and water flow. Rhythmic rocking of the boat does generate propulsion, but is forbidden by the rules when racing.

Mainsail Trim

Under light conditions, maximum propulsive force is what you want from the mainsail; pointing high is of secondary importance. With a mere breath of a breeze the closest you will get will be a full 10 degrees less than with a medium strength wind, particularly if there is a sea running. So, with the mast straight, the sail has to be set to belly. To do this, set up the luff with minimum halyard tension, so that the folds between luff and clew almost disappear. The foot should be slack enough to allow the lower part of the sail to achieve maximum camber.

The air flowing over the sail must be able to leave it smoothly at the leech, so this must be opened slightly. Ease the mainsheet to take pressure off the leech. Now, it can happen that in a very faint breeze there is not enough pressure applied to the sail to make the boom rise, because the weight of the boom and the downward pull of the sheet draw the leech taut. In that case it pays to move the traveller all the way to windward. The sheet pull on the boom is then at an angle; if a slight gust comes, the boom can rise more easily to open the leech. This action can be refined further by relieving the boom of any unnecessary weight; for instance, the kicking strap may be unshackled and some parts of the mainsheet unrove. If the wind strengthens, the leech must not be allowed to open further, so then the traveller has to go back to about amidships. However, if you are sailing with a Genoa with a lot of overlap, the traveller may stay up to windward; excessive opening of the leech is then prevented by hardening down on the kicking strap. Some sails have a through-batten near the head; in light airs this ought to be tied-in somewhat more tightly to make the upper part of the sail belly more.

Headsail Trim

Just like the mainsail, the headsail has to be trimmed to belly. First, the halyard is tightened only far enough for the first diagonal folds in the luff region to show up faintly. The second step concerns the sheet lead: if this is moved for'd a little, the sail bellies more — but also the leech closes more. Easing the sheet a little counters the latter. In particularly light airs, just the weight of the sheet may close the leech excessively; lightweight sheets reduce that effect. A forestay left a bit slack increases camber depth.

The end result of all the trimming efforts should be that the maximum camber depth has been moved to the centre of the sail.

Medium Strength Winds

In medium strength winds the boat can still be sailed upright enough without extreme changes of trim being necessary. The sails are set flatter by hauling the luffs more taut, care being taken once again to avoid folds appearing in the sail. This step applies primarily to narrow-beam yachts and when the water is relatively smooth; with more fully shaped hulls and if a sea is running that change of trim has to be delayed a bit longer.

Mainsail Trim

In smooth water the leech may almost be closed fully. The sail is now working with 100 percent efficiency. This closure is primarily achieved by means of strong pull on the sheet. The traveller is kept roughly amidships. Hardening down on the luff effects a reduction in camber and also moves it for'd. This produces a 'faster' but lower-energy profile. This faster profile is logical in that the air-flow over the sail has also speeded up. If the wind strengthens further, there has to be even more flattening — by increasing the mast bend. The boat now points at its best.

Headsail Trim

Like the mainsail, the headsail is trimmed flatter by tensioning the halyard more, and at the same time the sheet lead moved for'd for the light airs must be brought back again. A taut forestay plays a significant part in transferring for'd and reducing the sail camber. Whereas in light airs there is no harm in the forestay hanging a little slack to leeward, as the wind freshens it must be set up progressively harder. The less the slack, the better the boat will point.

Strong Winds

In strong winds the first commandment is to sail the boat with only the amount of heel permitted by its lines; that is the only way of exploiting the available speed potential to the full. In smooth water that means the sails have to be trimmed flat, opening progressively towards the head. If there is a sea running, they still have to be open but may belly a bit more. The important thing is to keep the wind pressure near the leech as low as possible to reduce the heel — and usually also weather-helm. The principal factor producing weather-helm is the wind pressure against the battened part of the mainsail. If in spite of all the flattening and opening trimming moves, too much heel or perhaps even a capsize (in dinghies) threatens, there is only one thing to do: ease the mainsheet generously at once. A well designed boat will carry on sailing fast enough even with the mainsail slatting all over, relying on the power of the headsail, but above all it will remain manoeuvrable.

In this connection, be warned of a frequently observed boat-handling error, which can jeopardise the safety of both boat and crew. If a particularly fierce squall hits the boat, leaving the mainsheet belayed and easing the foresheet somewhat is the wrong thing to do. The boat will head into the wind like a flash, carry on onto the other tack and end up hove-to, heeling hard over and with the headsail aback. You might then ship a lot of water into the cockpit and even down the companionway.

Mainsail Trim

To allow the sail to be trimmed as flat as possible, the mast must primarily be bent to the maximum amount. Minimum camber is attained when the battens are roughly parallel to the heading line of the boat; the minimum is exceeded if the battens flap over to leeward and the leech begins to slat — due to its being too open. By flattening the camber to the limit, the mainsail can be set flat into the wind almost like a board.

A sail flapping in the wind acts as a brake; a flat 'board', however, just stands edge-on to the wind. If that state of trim is achieved, only the headsail continues to drive the boat, with a drastic reduction in the heel. This possibility of trimming dead-flat has the advantage that during a brief sharp squall it may save you having to reef.

The luff is set up tight. You can do this using either the main halyard or the luff tensioner; by hauling the tensioner taut you additionally open the leech.

Sail pressure is reduced further if the traveller is pushed to leeward. That has the advantage that you do not need to ease the mainsheet. So you keep tension on the leech because the boom end does not rise; the upper part of the sail does not open too far. This trimming move is advantageous if it is not blowing too hard. But if you are sailing with an overlapping Genoa — a frequent practice of racing boats — then that move with the traveller will result in a large counterbelly in the mainsail. This can, however, be neutralised to some extent by careful trimming of the headsail.

Positioning the traveller to leeward means that the boat will point less well, but in the case of planing dinghies that often does not matter; not pointing as well as possible, but rather sailing upright and fast are what matters when it is blowing hard.

The traveller operating line should always be to windward and to hand. Should a hefty gust arrive the traveller can be eased at once and be hauled back again when the wind drops. Strong and gusting winds prove who is a good helmsman. With an expert steering, the heel of the boat remains substantially constant, regardless of whether there is a squall howling through the rigging or there is just a reasonable blow in between. Pressure on the sails, particularly on the mainsail, must be kept at the same level, and it is this which requires constant work with the traveller and also the mainsheet.

If a hard blow is combined with a relatively heavy sea, the lower part of the mainsail should be set a bit fuller — achieved by easing clew outhaul and luff tensioner a little. However, if the boat will not sail upright any more, you must reef. Better a reefed full sail than an unreefed flattened one.

Headsail Trim
If it is blowing hard, the headsail also has to be trimmed flat and more open in the upper region. Of prime importance is a taut fore-

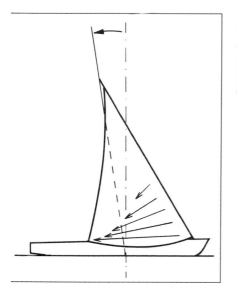

Increased mast rake creates an automatic opening of the Genoa leech; a welcome form of 'sheet-lead adjustment' if there is a lot of wind.

stay and the luff set up hard. Some headsails have a small luff tensioner worked into the tack; that can also be used to flatten the profile.

If in spite of the headsail being trimmed flat a boat cannot be sailed upright enough any more, the leech must be opened; for example, by moving the sheet leads aft or, using Barber haulers. This means the upper part of the sail will scarcely draw any more, but that does not matter — what is important is that the sail's centre of effort is lowered and you can thus sail more upright.

Yet another effect is achieved with this trim. Opening the leech makes it easier for the back wind to escape from the sail; it does not strike the mainsail so hard and helps it set better. Opening the leech can also be achieved in another way: the sheet leads stay where they are, and the mast rake is increased instead.

Finally, there is a more or less involuntary way of achieving this trim, namely by the natural stretch of the sailcloth. This wind-dependent, totally automatic opening of the headsail is hard to allow for, and can only be mastered by dint of individual observation.

In heavy seas the rule is that a somewhat fuller jib pulls better than a Genoa trimmed flat.

Trim for Reaching

Light Airs

The trim for head and mainsails does not differ significantly from that for beating. Both sails are set a bit fuller, for the target is maximum propulsive power; the 'pointing' factor is eliminated. To reduce the resistance of the underwater hull the stern of the boat in particular should be relieved of load, so the crew must be especially effective in trimming the boat down by the bow.

Mainsail Trim
Maximum camber is attained with the mast not just trimmed upright but indeed bent 'negatively'; i.e. with a convex curvature towards the stern and the masthead inclined for'd. A mast trimmed in this odd fashion may look peculiar, but in this case the end justifies the means.

The luff may be eased until the first diagonal creases become visible — maximum camber is more important than appearance. The same applies to the foot. These folds, perpendicular to the air flow, must however not be allowed to have a braking effect. The leech must remain near to closed. Since the sheet no longer pulls vertically on the boom, thus controlling the opening of the leech, the kicking strap has to take over. This trim technique starts in light airs; getting this near-to-closed effect calls for a delicate touch. Here also the tell-tales at the leech are a help. The traveller position is not important.

Headsail Trim
A particularly deep camber is achieved by letting the forestay sag and easing the halyard. It is permissible for the first creases to appear in the luff region. At the same time the sheet lead needs to be moved for'd and outboard.

Medium Strength Winds

Mainsail Trim
As the wind strengthens, the function of the main boom kicking strap becomes more important. The leech must remain near to closed, particularly in smooth water. On a close reach, many straps are ineffective owing to stretch or not being set up hard enough. On such a course, their job may be taken over by the mainsheet if there is an extra-long traveller and it is moved right to the leeward end. If the wind is for'd of the beam, you can continue sailing with the increased mast rake; the advantages reduce progressively as the wind moves aft of the beam. The mast must then be trimmed upright again.

For as long as the boat can be sailed upright enough without any trouble, the mast may be left trimmed 'negatively'. When that ceases to be the case, the sail has to be flattened somewhat and the mast brought upright.

Headsail Trim
The camber setting is the same as for light airs, but the halyard may have to be set up a bit harder to prevent excessive creasing in the luff region. Sheet lead — no change.

Strong Winds

Provided the safety of the yacht or dinghy is ensured, the sails may well be left in high-energy trim: i.e. full and closed. It is up to the helmsman to avoid any broaches to windward or, even worse, to leeward. But if it comes on to blow hard, a compromise has to be reached between optimum trim and boat safety. It is up to individual crews to decide which side of the compromise they want to come down on, in the conditions prevailing. It means anyway that energy has to be taken out of the sails by trimming them flatter and more open. Important though correct trim is, continuous adjustment of the sheets is much more decisive for safe and speedy progress.

Running a boat safely also involves a continuous watch on the area of water to windward. Sharp squalls can usually be recognised in time, and once the danger has been identified easing the sheets smartly and in advance presents no problem. The best way of dealing with such squalls is to bear away and ease the sheets quick as you can.

Mainsail Trim

In strong winds the kicking strap assumes a dominant role, deciding as it does substantially how the sail sets. The foot may be set up hard. Avoiding excessive heel is more important than trying to generate surplus energy. If it becomes almost impossible to control the boat, even the strap may be eased a little, particularly in boats with an especially long boom. If these heel strongly to leeward with the boom well out, the boom end will drag heavily in the water. In larger boats a powerful moment builds up and the boom may break. Dinghies swing to leeward about the end and may capsize.

To prevent such calamitous effects the strap has to be let go entirely at once; the control line must therefore be within the crew's reach and quickly releasable. The same applies to the mainsheet, which should be in experienced hands.

Headsail Trim
The trim corresponds to that for medium strength winds. Particularly where there is an overlapping Genoa, in squalls the leech has to be opened wide by easing the sheet, without allowing the sail to flap too wildly. This also avoids an excessive counterbelly in the mainsail.

Trim For Running

Light Airs

The camber settings for both sails for running do not differ significantly from those for reaching.

Mainsail Trim
To trim the sail particularly full, indeed even baggy like a spinnaker, the leech line is set up really hard, the kicking strap having been eased a little. The mast should be upright, or even inclined for'd a bit. Boats with a long main boom are heeled to windward a little, to move the sail area upwards somewhat into the undisturbed airflow. A typical trim, to be observed on Star-boats or Finn-dinghies.

Headsail Trim
If the headsail is pushed out to windward with a spinnaker pole, this should be trimmed horizontal and pulled to windward as far as possible to achieve a large projected area. Leech and foot tension should be about the same. If the leech is closed too far, the wind will escape from the open foot; if, on the other hand, the foot is set up too hard, the upper part of the leech will twist too much and the wind escape forward out of it without doing any work.

Medium Strength Winds

Mainsail Trim
The camber setting corresponds to that for running in light airs. To exclude any possibility of the leech opening too far, the kicking strap must be set up hard. When doing this, do not forget to ease the leech line (hauled tight for light airs) in time.

Headsail Trim
This is no different from that which is correct for light airs.

Strong Winds

The wrong trim and a poor helmsman can turn this point of sailing into a nightmare, especially if there is a lot of rough water about. Any boat will then tend to yaw violently, i.e. turn and roll uncontrollably and strongly alternately to windward and leeward.

To counteract this, three things are important. Firstly, the boat has to be trimmed down by the stern. This steadies it because the after portion, due to broader beam at the waterline, produces more stability than the slim forebody. Secondly, the helmsman must act as follows: if the boat begins to heel to windward he must luff at once; if to leeward, bear away correspondingly. Only rapid reaction plus anticipatory and forceful counter-steering will allow the yaw to be mastered.

If a spinnaker is set, this will reinforce the see-saw motion of the boat by swinging to and fro. A rule-of-thumb is always to steer to follow the spinnaker. Since it pulls the mast now to port, now to starboard, the swinging spinnaker is always just a shade ahead of the boat's movements. The helmsman can react even more swiftly.

The third point concerns the mainsail trim, as follows.

Mainsail Trim
The first essential is to set the kicking strap bar-taut, so that the leech remains totally closed. Only this trim can counteract yawing. Even if the boom rises only a little, the leech opens immediately; the head region flies forward and windward forces are

These three '420' dinghies, running before a strong wind, have set up their kicking straps hard. This is a safeguard against capsizing.

generated. Gone is the steadying effect of the leech. The sail camber remains deep.

Headsail Trim

The spinnaker pole should be pulled far to windward to trim the headsail flat. If it is trimmed too full because the boom-end is too far for'd, it will start swinging with the wave motion and thus reinforce the yawing. The sheet lead can be pushed right for'd; the sheet then acts broadly like a spinnaker pole downhaul. The pole moves about less.

Masthead Rig

The masthead rig has the forestay, standing backstay, and upper shrouds secured to the masthead. Because of the high tensile forces from the stays and the compressive stress these set up in the mast, this has to be especially flexurally strong over its entire length — from head to foot. Unlike the practice usual with $\frac{7}{8}$ rigs, it may therefore not taper towards the head. Consequently masts for masthead rigs are of the same section throughout and accordingly can be bent only within narrow limits. For the sailmaker, this means that he has to cut the mainsail flatter than he would for a $\frac{7}{8}$ rig.

The typical assembly of stays for a masthead-rig mast comprises:

- two upper shrouds
- forestay and standing backstay
- two fore lower shrouds (or a baby stay)
- two aft lower shrouds.

This assembly creates no handling problems and is considered particularly rough-weather-worthy.

The upper-shroud chainplates are roughly abreast the mast; those of the aft lower shrouds are mounted aft of them and those of

The babystay tension is determined by the position of the slider on the track. If this is pulled to the left, the babystay pulls the spreader-region of the mast forward; the mainsail sets flatter.

the fore lower shrouds, for'd. Sometimes a baby stay is rigged instead of the two fore lower shrouds; this attaches at spreader level and is taken to a centreline point on the foredeck or the for'd cabin bulkhead. Fore lower shrouds or a baby stay fulfil the same function: both see to it that the mast is pulled forward in the spreader region.

When anchoring a baby stay to the deck, one must see to it that the high tensile load does not lift the deck or even damage it. A baby stay simplifies the array of stays — you do save one stay — but complicates changing over the headsail when going about because sheets and sail chafe against the stay and slow down the manoeuvre. But this disadvantage can be eliminated by means of a plastic tube about 1.5 m. long, obtainable from the plumbing trade. You just fit this over the baby stay so that sheets and sail can slide past it more easily and with less damage. This sort of plastic tube can also be fitted over the fore lower shrouds, against which sheets and sail will also chafe. There is less of this problem with the upper shrouds.

Basic Trim of the Mast

After stepping the mast, the stays/shrouds are all bent on without tensioning them, before basic trimming starts. The length of the forestay is determined first. If mast rake is to be increased, toggles have to be fitted between rigging screw and chainplate. Once the stay has been secured, the upper shrouds can be set up. The evenness of this setting up (i.e. the uprightness of the mast in the athwartship direction) is easy enough to check: the main halyard is eased until the shackle just touches, say, the side deck on the starboard side near the upper shroud chainplate. Having belayed the halyard, you then bring the shackle to the corresponding position on the port side. Should the distance from the deck be different, this indicates that the mast is tilted and this must be corrected at once.

The lower shrouds attach at spreader level. If the aft ones are eased and the fore ones set up hard, the mast is pulled forward in the spreader region; it bends. With extremes of bending, the masthead is pulled down a little again. The upper shrouds have to be set up harder to avoid the head dipping to leeward in strong winds and slackening the forestay.

Finally the standing-backstay tensioner is used to regulate the forestay tension. The correct basic trim has been achieved if the mast, without any sails being set, is pre-bent aft slightly. This is necessary because a well set-up headsail halyard will pull the masthead upright again, so without this pre-bend the mast would be bent the wrong way. Result: the mainsail would set unduly full; the leech close too much. That trim is a frequently encountered reason for strong weather helm, because the wind presses excessively strongly against the battened portion and thereby generates a windward moment.

The trim set in harbour must be rechecked when sailing in a fresh breeze, particularly when close hauled. If the masthead then

The standing backstay of a masthead-rigged mast requires an especially powerful tensioning device. Tackles are generally of no use because you cannot get enough pull on them. The tensioner shown has two folding handles for operating it.

If the rig involves two standing backstays, it may be possible on one of the smaller yachts to produce enough forestay tension even with a tensioning arrangement (tackle) such as this.

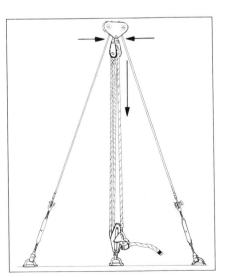

bends to windward, the lower shrouds have to be set up harder; if to leeward, it is the upper ones that are slack.

Since on a masthead-rigged boat the headsails are relatively larger than on a $\frac{7}{8}$ rig, these sails must be especially carefully trimmed.

Light Airs Trim

Beating
To trim the mainsail full, the mast is trimmed straight by slackening the lower shrouds and reducing the standing-backstay tension. The latter action also makes the forestay sag a bit, giving the Genoa a fuller set.

Reaching
The trim is similar to that close-hauled, but additionally the aft lower shrouds may be hauled very taut to bend the mast negatively and so give a particularly full set to the mainsail. Further slackening of the standing backstay will also let the Genoa luff sag further to leeward so that the Genoa camber is now a maximum.

Medium Strength Wind Trim

Beating
The fuller the cut of the sail, the harder the fore lower shrouds are set up, in order to pull the fullness out of the sail. Furthermore the standing backstay has to be tautened, to increase the mast bend and above all to tighten the forestay. Now the Genoa luff no longer sags as much as it did; its camber is reduced.

Reaching
To maximise mainsail fullness, the aft lower shrouds have to be tensioned, and the standing backstay is loosened to trim the Genoa as full as possible.

Strong Wind Trim

Beating

To maximise the mast bend and tension the forestay as far as possible, the fore lower shrouds have to be set up particularly hard and the standing backstay tensioned 'right to the top'. The limit is reached when the mainsail is trimmed flat enough. The mast bend must always be harmonised with the curvature of the sail luff. If there is a sea running, great care must be taken to prevent the mast having too much freedom of movement in the spreader region, so the lower shrouds must be kept in tension. First the fore ones have to be set up, then the aft ones. If this is not done large movements (oscillations) can develop in this region and can finally lead to a compression fracture of the mast.

When you have finished sailing, take the tension off the rigging to ease the strain on the boat's structure.

Reaching

For as long as the boat remains safe to handle, the trim recommended for medium strength winds can be retained. But if it begins to blow harder, the mainsail has to be flattened by tensioning the standing backstay more and setting up the fore lower shrouds harder.

The $\frac{7}{8}$ or Fractional Rig with Swept-back Spreaders

The $\frac{7}{8}$ rig has the forestay attached to the mast below the head. The mathematical expression '$\frac{7}{8}$' nowadays has only historical significance. It derives from the 'Kreuzer-Renn' (KR) formula for seagoing cruisers used many years ago in Germany. This national racing handicap formula favoured the forestay attachment point at $\frac{7}{8}$ of the total mast height; i.e. $\frac{1}{8}$ down from the head. Nowadays one still talks of a $\frac{7}{8}$ or fractional rig whatever the height on the mast at which the forestay attaches. Designations such as $\frac{13}{14}$ or $\frac{11}{12}$ are not usual, even if considered mathematically to be the precise height at which the forestay attaches.

The advantage of the fractional rig over the masthead rig lies in the increased flexibility of the mast, which permits much more effective adjustment of the mainsail profile to the different wind and wave conditions. The trimming band width is increased; correspondingly the mainsail can be set much fuller, improving the light-airs characteristics. On the other hand, the increased bendability of the mast also allows the sail to be trimmed flatter, and thus the camber to be reduced, in stronger winds. That improves the rough-weather characteristics.

Masts for fractional rigs are, as a rule, tapered towards the head, thus making it easier to pull them aft by means of high tension in the standing backstay. Where the mast tapers strongly, this pull particularly affects its upper part, so the mainsail is trimmed flat in its upper regions and the leech opened. This lowers the centre of pressure of the sail; the boat can be sailed more upright.

Masts with less taper react differently to increased tension in the standing backstay. The bend in the upper part is less pronounced; the pull of the backstay is distributed over the whole length of the mast — i.e. also on the lower portion. The bending curve is more even over the length. If the sailmaker is to produce an optimally tailored mainsail, he must know all about the mast's bend characteristics. Only then can he match the curvature of the luff — and thus the camber of the sail — to the mast bend. To this end the maximum bend of the mast must be established.

Basic Trim of the Mast

After stepping the mast, all stays and shrouds are bent on first without tension, then basic trimming starts. As regards mast rake, it is the same as for the masthead rig. Once the rake has been settled, tensioning of the upper shrouds can begin. Under tension, these apply pressure from both sides to the spreaders. Since these are swept back, this pressure is transmitted to the mast at an angle, i.e. slanting forwards. So the mast is pushed forwards in the spreader region; it bends backwards. The harder the upper shrouds are set up, the more the mast bends. Also affecting the amount of bend is the degree of sweep-back of the spreaders (spreader angle).

If the spreaders have no sweep-back, it is impossible to apply any forward pressure to the mast in the spreader region. Result: the mast would not bend. The more pronounced the spreader sweep-back, the greater the pressure exerted on the mast and the greater the mast bend. The bend also increases with spreader length, because this increases the effectiveness of the shrouds' pressure component on the spreaders. Spreaders projecting too far, however, have the disadvantage that the Genoa cannot be sheeted in to achieve close-hauled pointing ability.

Before applying maximum tension to the upper shrouds, the

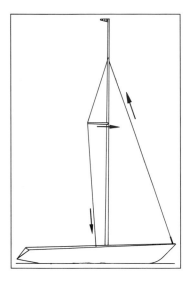

High tension in the upper shrouds produces a taut forestay and mast pre-bend in the spreader region.

standing backstay should be set up hard. This bends the mast, and the shrouds' attachment point moves down a bit; they become slack, therefore setting them up becomes much easier. Above all they are well tensioned once the backstay is eased.

To have proper control of the mast bend (pre-bend) produced by the upper shrouds, there must be lower shrouds. The chainplates for these, like those for the upper shrouds, are fastened to the hull aft of the mast. The lower shrouds pull the spreader-region of the mast towards the stern; without them, that region of the mast would break away forwards. The more the lower shrouds are tensioned, the straighter the mast will be fore and aft. To see if the mast is also straight athwartships, check by looking up the mast groove. This check should be made when the rig is not carrying sails and also on a beat in a fresh breeze.

With fractional rigs and running backstays, forestay tension is applied via the windward backstay; in the absence of these it must be applied via the upper shrouds and the standing backstay. The more the upper shrouds are tensioned, the more rigid the forestay will become, since the slanting-aft pull of the shrouds also pulls the top of the forestay aft.

If the rudder blade is transom hung the standing backstay tensioner must be divided.

A powerful standing backstay tensioner on a 7/8 rigged 9m boat.

Light Airs Trim

Beating
The mast is set upright by tensioning the lower shrouds and easing the standing backstay. The mainsail sets full. If there is a sea running, the leech can easily be opened by re-tensioning the backstay; an even deeper set can be obtained by tensioning the lower shroud further.

Reaching
Maximum mainsail fullness results from setting up the lower shrouds particularly hard. The standing backstay must be slacked back for this; that makes a 'negative' mast bend possible. Since as a

rule the upper-shroud tension remains constant, the forestay also remains taut. Thus there is a limit to how full the headsail can be trimmed.

Medium Strength Wind Trim

Beating
To flatten the mainsail, the lower shrouds are eased until the mast is straight or, should the wind strengthen further, bends very slightly aft. By setting the standing backstay more or less taut, the weather-helm effect of the wind pressure on mainsail leech can be influenced. This step must thus be correlated with the heel of the boat.

Reaching
For as long as the boat can be sailed upright enough, the light-airs trim may well be maintained. If the wind strengthens, the standing backstay has to be tightened a bit to open the leech more. As the wind increases, the lower shrouds may be eased as appropriate, to give the mast a slight backward bend.

Strong Wind Trim

Beating
Mainsail camber is reduced by high tension in the standing backstay and extensively eased lower shrouds, giving the mast its maximum bend. The high backstay tension at the same time ensures a taut forestay so that the headsail also is automatically trimmed flatter.

Reaching
If the boat develops too much weather-helm the mainsail must be trimmed progressively flatter by easing the lower shrouds and heaving in a bit on the standing backstay. The lower shrouds are trimmed as described for the masthead rig.

Looking up the groove: the shrouds have been tensioned evenly, the mast is straight.

Watch out! In rough weather, particularly if combined with heavy seas, faulty mast trim may result in the mast breaking.

By virtue of the taut cloth, an unreefed mainsail trimmed flat gives the mast a measure of support; it limits possible oscillations in the fore and aft direction. With a heavily reefed mainsail, however, that support is lacking in the upper mast region. That portion can thus oscillate more freely, only the masthead being pulled aft by the backstay. If now the mainsheet is sheeted in hard, a lot of tension is applied to the leech and transferred to the head of the sail, which is somewhere between spreader and forestay top. The pull of the sheet thus brings this part of the mast aft and downwards, counteracting the pre-bend of the mast.

Well set upper shrouds would ensure that the bend is maintained and would absorb the forces due to this new static situation without difficulty. However, if the shrouds are only moderately taut, the pre-bend is only moderately stabilised. It can become unstable if the boat slams heavily into a wave. This means that the mast starts to oscillate in the fore and aft direction and finally produces a reverse bend in the spreader region. Such a violent action would spring the spreader ends suddenly forward; deformation or indeed fracture results near the spreader roots, and the mast breaks. Such a breakdown is entirely preventable, the important factor being to make the mast pre-bend as stable as possible. The following trimming steps are required:

1. The upper shrouds must be set up really hard.
2. The lower shrouds must be eased extensively.
3. The kicking strap must be shortened right down so that the boom pushes the mast forward strongly.
4. The standing backstay must be set up hard.

The $\frac{7}{8}$ or Fractional Rig with Running Backstays

This rig, mostly used for racing yachts, has the following distinctive features:

- Forestay and upper shrouds attach below the masthead.
- Upper and lower shrouds fasten to chainplates mounted roughly abreast the mast.
- Spreaders are in a straight line, i.e. not swept back.
- Running backstays attach to the mast at forestay-attachment level.

This rig offers more sail trim potential than that with swept spreaders and is arguably the most flexible solution currently available to maximise the effectiveness of the mainsail in particular. Not only can the mast be bent more, it is also possible to alter the mast rake while sailing.

Tensioning the forestay of a fractional rig with swept-back spreaders is achieved by tensioning the upper shrouds. This works quite well, but nothing like as well as with running backstays. The principal function of these is to set up the forestay; additionally

An important function of the running backstays is to set the forestay up hard.

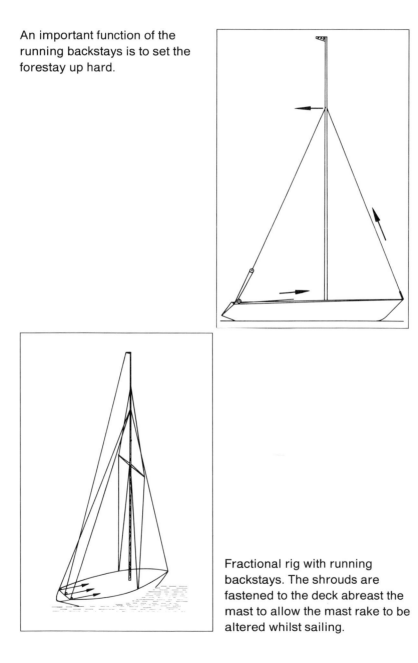

Fractional rig with running backstays. The shrouds are fastened to the deck abreast the mast to allow the mast rake to be altered whilst sailing.

they reinforce the mast bend. Since they are slanted aft to somewhere near the stern, the forestay can be set up particularly hard.

I am not going to conceal the disadvantage of running backstays: they are extremely operator-unfriendly, especially for a small, cruising orientated crew. Because running backstays require exact and swift handling, anyone ignoring that requirement in a strengthening wind must also reckon with an increasing risk of the mast breaking.

The difficulties can, however, be counteracted if the mast section is stiff enough. A little aft of the shroud chainplates, additional plates or eyebolts are fixed to the side decks. The lower end of each stay is connected to a small tackle, which in turn is shackled to one of these additional plates. Setting up these tackles hard ensures the forestay is reasonably taut, even though if the direction of pull is not ideal it is sufficient to prevent the mast breaking.

Running backstays are predominantly operated on one of two principles. For setting up on small boats (up to about 8 m. long) tackles are used; on larger yachts, two-speed winches are usual. When employing tackles, there is a proven system which allows coarse and fine adjustment to be handled separately. The coarse adjustment is used when a large change is required, for example when gybing or if the mainsheet is eased suddenly. The fine adjustment is for setting up the windward stay when sailing closehauled. This system works as follows: the wire stay from the mast ends about one metre from the deck near the stern, and has a block fitted to this end. Through this block a rope is rove, one end of which goes via a turning block near the transom to a cleat in the cockpit (coarse adjustment). The other end of this two-part tackle is in turn attached to a multi-purchase tackle whose standing block is also near the stern and whose hauling part goes to a second cleat in the cockpit (fine adjustment). (See Illustration opp.) Both cleats must be quickly reachable and easy to operate. The system carries a risk in that a cleat may fail unintentionally.

With this type of rig, the mast-bend can also be adjusted by means of the kicking strap. The trimming effect on the lower part of the mast depends on the distance from the gooseneck to the mast heel on a deck-mounted mast, or to the mast gate on a keel-stepped

Two arrangements for setting up the running backstays: either by means of a winch (A) or using two tackles with coarse and fine adjustment (B). The latter is usual for smaller boats.

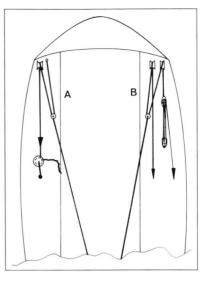

mast. The greater this distance, the more the mast bends forward around the gooseneck under the pressure from the hauled-taut kicking strap via the boom.

If the lower part of the mast is to be bent by this means, care must be taken to prevent the leech closing too much. The standing backstay may have to be tightened to open it again.

Basic Trim of the Mast

Since the shroud mountings are abreast the mast, they do not influence the mast bend in the fore and aft direction. They only secure it athwartships, a point easily checked by looking up the mast groove. The upper shrouds are set as for the rig with the swept-back spreaders, using the standing backstay tensioner set up hard. The choice of mast rake is arbitrary, since it can be altered later, whilst under sail. If the masthead bends to windward, the windward lower shroud needs setting up harder; if to leeward, it is the windward upper shroud that is too slack.

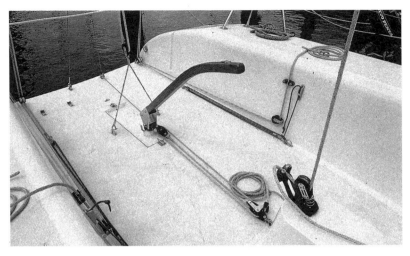

Important trimming lines such as standing backstay tensioner, running backstay coarse and fine adjusters, and mainsheet are easy to reach on this Fractional rig boat ('Fun'). A traveller is dispensed with.

Light Airs Trim

Beating
The mast is trimmed upright by easing the standing backstay, to maximise mainsail camber. Only a little tension is applied to the Genoa luff by slight tensioning of the running backstay. This allows the Genoa to belly.

Reaching
The mast trim is the same as for beating. The windward running backstay can be eased further to make the Genoa camber especially deep.

On this fractional-rig boat (J24) the backstay tensioner can be worked from both sides of the cockpit. The cleats are just for'd of the traveller.

Medium Strength Wind Trim

Beating
Since this rig allows almost infinite trimming variety it must be worked at constantly. To reduce the sail camber, the standing backstay tension is increased. If the mainsail lower portion is cut very full, the main boom kicking-strap can be set up hard. The windward running backstay must be set up hard to flatten the headsail also. Mast rake may be increased, especially if there is a sea running.

Reaching
The sail camber is set substantially as for light airs, but the windward running backstay has to be set up a bit harder to reduce the tendency of the mast to swivel about its heel. If the boat starts to

take charge, the standing backstay needs to be hardened up slightly. Unless the wind is from too far aft, the increased mast rake may be retained.

Strong Wind Trim

Beating
Windward running backstay, standing backstay and main boom kicking-strap are all set up as hard as possible to trim the sails flat. Should the mainsail be reefed, stability of the mast pre-bend must be absolutely ensured so that the mast cannot break, especially if there is a sea running. If the wind drops, the standing backstay may be eased again a bit, to increase the mainsail propulsive power.

Reaching
The trim corresponds to that for medium-strength wind, except that the windward running backstay has to be hardened up more to reduce the mast working in a seaway. If a spinnaker pole is carried, the main boom kicking-strap must be left set up hard, otherwise the spinnaker pole pressure against the mast may break it.

Dinghy Rig with Swept-back Spreaders

With this type of rig there are many more factors affecting mast bend than in the case of the $\frac{7}{8}$ (fractional) or masthead rigs on bigger boats. Furthermore they partially interact. To deal with the interaction of all the factors influencing trim, to evaluate them, and finally from this to compile foolproof trimming instructions is next to impossible. The subject is too complex and represents an almost inexhaustible topic for discussion. The aspects covered in this book cannot therefore be either comprehensive or absolute, but it is possible to pass on valuable tips to allow basic trimming under a variety of conditions to be undertaken without too many mistakes being made.

As a matter of principle, both crew and sailmaker must see to it that the cut of the sails, particularly the mainsail, matches the mast bend. Thus, however correct it may be generally to flatten the mainsail in winds of medium strength and above, due to the mast curvature (if that has already opened the leech), the luff tensioner must not be tensioned, otherwise all power will be lost. So, in medium to strong winds keep off the Cunningham. A few creases in the luff are of only secondary importance here; much more important is that the camber corresponds to the ambient conditions.

The dinghy mast bending curve is influenced by the following factors:

- mast section, method of construction
- length and angle of spreaders
- rig tension
- kicking-strap tension
- mast control
- mainsheet angle of pull

Mast Section

The stiffer a mast is, the less it will bend, and the longer the mainsail will continue to belly in a strengthening wind. A sail that bellies and whose leech is closed produces more heel than one trimmed flat. So a stiff mast suits a heavy crew, which by virtue of its body weight can keep a dinghy sailing upright even in a fresh wind. A more lightweight crew usually needs a more flexible mast. Its timely bending automatically flattens the mainsail and opens the leech, particularly near the head. This reduces the wind loading on the upper part of the mainsail, and it therefore takes less crew weight to trim the dinghy upright.

The choice of mast section also depends on where you are going to sail. On an inland lake with relatively smooth water, a stiff mast makes sense because in smooth waters the leech can remain closed for longer. In a wave-prone coastal region, on the other hand, it is advantageous if the top of the mast flexes in the seaway and the leech can adjust to the high alternating stresses generated by that seaway. It opens when heavily stressed, i.e. under heavy pressure near the head, and closes again automatically when that pressure is reduced on the back of a wave. An even propulsive force results, since the airflow can follow the line of the mainsail camber better and more harmoniously. There is less flow breakaway at the leech. Lastly, it is easier to keep the dinghy sailing more upright by virtue of the flexing and thus damping effect of the masthead, because the load peaks are removed from the top part of the sail.

Spreaders

These must be mounted in such a way that they cannot flex sufficiently to allow their tips to move forward of the mast, so there must be a stop or a rigid mounting to prevent any oscillating movement of the mast in the spreader region. Furthermore, for optimum absorption of the shroud forces each spreader should be at right angles to an imaginary straight line, from where the shroud adjoins the mast to the chainplate. If that angle is wrong, a moment is set up and the spreader could slide up or down on the shroud.

Spreader length is one of the factors determining mast bend. Long spreaders stiffen the head region of the mast; wind force will not bend this so far to leeward. The mainsail leech opens less. Correspondingly, short spreaders permit more bending of the masthead region; this reduces the load on the upper part of the sail and it is easier to sail the dinghy upright.

Spreader angle determines the backward-bending behaviour of the mast: the more the spreaders are swept back, the more the tension in the shrouds pushes the mast forward. The mainsail is flattened in good time and the leech opens.

A heavy crew, able to keep its dinghy trimmed upright well into fresh conditions, is thus better advised to have spreaders with little sweep-back. For a lightweight crew, unable to keep a dinghy sufficiently upright in stronger winds, timely mast flexure to windward and aft is a good thing. That assumes that the rig is set up hard, because only then do the spreaders have a bending effect.

Rig Tension

High rig tension is not only needed to bend the mast, it also ensures high forestay tension. In most dinghies the jib halyard is used to tension the rig; the harder that is set up, the more tension is transferred to the rig and thus also to the shrouds. The presence of a forestay then merely ensures that the mast does not come down if, for instance, the jib halyard should part.

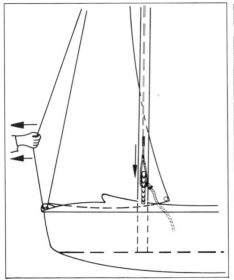

Where there is no jib halyard tensioner, the halyard can nevertheless be set up taut by pulling hard on the forestay and at the same time belaying the end of the wire halyard.

An exemplary jib halyard tensioner for dinghies. The wire halyard is taken directly to a lever tensioner.

Kicking Strap

Setting up the kicking strap hard causes the mast to bend predominantly in the lower region. Since the strap additionally controls the tautness of the leech, high strap tension also closes it. Unlike the fractional rig, the leech can then no longer be opened by hauling taut the standing backstay; only the mast bend in the head region can then achieve that opening.

Setting up the kicking strap
especially hard can significantly
influence the trim of the mast.

Mast Control

The function of mast control is to limit the amount of bend in the
lower part of the mast. The less the mast can be deflected forward
where it passes through the deck, the less its bend.

To achieve this, a wide range of techniques can be used, rang-
ing from simple wooden shims inserted into the deck aperture for'd
of the mast, to lower shrouds attached at gooseneck level and cap-
able of adjustment even whilst under sail. Also quite usual are
adjustable-length rods, mast struts, supporting the mast at an
angle from for'd. Mast control acting at gooseneck level —
whether from for'd or from aft — takes the load from the main
boom directly; it is therefore particularly effective for controlling
the mast bend — even if the kicking strap is set up hard, such as
with the wind hard on the quarter.

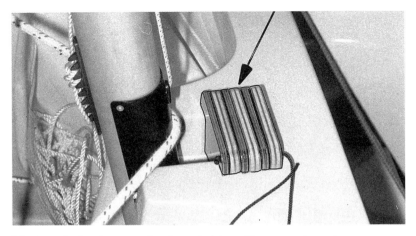

Mast control using wooden-board shims. The more boards are inserted in the deck aperture, the straighter the mast remains.

Mast strut. By turning the little wheel just above the deck, the length of the rod is varied. The longer the rod is made, the more the mast is pushed aft.

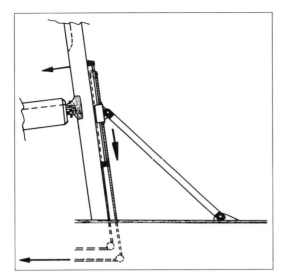

A mast strut whose angle to the deck can be varied. The rod's upper end is connected to a slider movable on a rail.

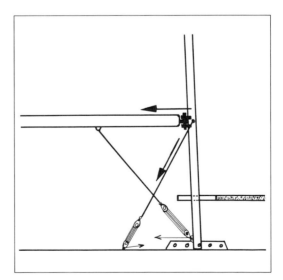

Mast control by adjustable lower shrouds.

Mainsheet Angle of Pull

If the sheet pulls vertically on the boom, the latter will not be pulled either for'd or aft, but if the point of attachment on the boom is moved aft, the boom will be pulled for'd. Useful if the kicking strap has to be left slack but you want to trim the lower part of the sail a bit flatter by bending the mast more.

Basic Trim of the Mast

After the mast has been stepped, the rake must first of all be determined. The more rake required, the further down the perforated-bar should the shrouds be connected. In the case of boats whose shrouds can be adjusted whilst under sail, this decision can be reached later.

Watch out! Extreme rake has the mast heel canted in the step; it may therefore jump out of this with its forward edge. So: either saw the heel off at an angle or use an especially secure mast mounting.

Normally the mast stands in a step and is taken through a deck aperture. This must be so narrow that the mast has no sideways play; too wide an aperture allows the mast to bend sideways uncontrollably, which is harmful.

Tensioning of the shrouds is achieved — as already mentioned — by means of the jib halyard, using either a tackle or a lever tensioner. If the class regulations do not allow help from such tensioners there is a proven method for setting up the luff line and the shrouds. First, the headsail is set; hanks may be dispensed with on this occasion. The foresheet hand now pulls the forestay wire powerfully forward; this also pulls forward the forestay fitting on the mast. The shrouds are tensioned; the jib halyard goes slack. The latter is then set up again and its end belayed on a hooked bar. When the forestay is released, the whole pull comes onto the wire inside the luff seam. The tension in the cloth of the luff can often be adjusted with a headsail Cunningham, independently of the tension in the wire — which means that even with the wire set up hard the luff can be left relatively slack.

If the mast has too much lateral clearance in the deck aperture, its middle portion will bend to leeward.

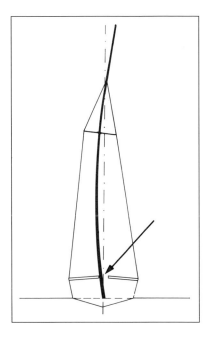

Light Airs Trim

Beating

The mainsail trim depends very much on its cut, but above all on the size of the headsail. If you are sailing with a scarcely overlapping jib, then the mainsail can be trimmed fuller, because the back wind from the jib barely strikes the mainsail. So the mast must be set up straight, which means:

● Rig tension must be kept low so that the upper shrouds do not apply any pressure to the spreaders, and any unwanted pre-bend is thus avoided.

● The mast control system must push the mast far enough back to eliminate any remaining pre-bend in the lower region.

● The kicking strap should be slack.

However, if you are sailing with an extensively overlapping Genoa, then the for'd, lower part of the mainsail has to be flattened more. Otherwise the backwind from the Genoa would be 'pinched' in the slot between Genoa and mainsail. This trim change is primarily achieved by increasing the rig tension; also by moving the mainsheet block on the boom further aft. Theoretically, setting up the kicking strap hard would also do the trick, but the leech would then be too far closed. Only if the wind freshens will it open again, because of the masthead bending.

By means of low rig tension, in very light airs one can achieve some sag in the forestay and thus a fuller set headsail.

Reaching

A particularly deep mainsail camber is achieved if the mast control system is made to push the mast aft particularly powerfully, and rig tension is reduced some more. True, this increases forestay tension somewhat, but the compromise is nevertheless worthwhile. Kicking-strap tension closes the leech.

Medium Strength Wind Trim

Beating

For as long as you can sail upright, the leech may be left closed, but as the wind strengthens so the sails have to be set flatter by means of the following steps:

- increasing the rig tension further
- reducing the mast control effect
- setting up the kicking strap hard

The extent of these measures depends on the cut of the mainsail and the weight of the crew. The increased rig tension automatically trims the headsail flatter.

Reaching

First of all the kicking strap has to be set up hard until the leech is almost completely closed. The mast is pushed so far aft by the control system that its lower part stands dead upright.

A bend in the upper part can be achieved by a slight reduction of the shroud tension; this also ensures a slight sag of the forestay.

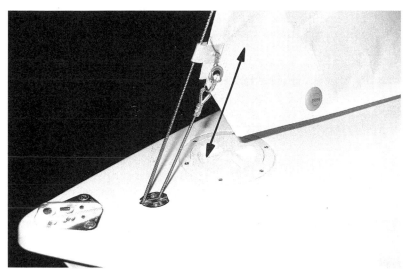

This wire luff tensioner is taken through the deck to a tackle whose hauling part is led to the cockpit.

Strong Wind Trim

Beating

If before the start of a race you can see that there is going to be a lot of wind, you can increase the spreader sweep-back while still on shore. Available commercially but little used is a spreader mounting which permits variation of the angle even while sailing. The inner ends of the two spreaders are connected to operating lines run inside the mast to a tensioning arrangement in the cockpit.

After the shrouds have been set up to give the maximum mast rake, the jib halyard is first of all set up hard, which produces a high degree of mast pre-bend. Yet more mast bend can be achieved by easing-up on the mast control and setting the kicking strap up hard. If pronounced diagonal folds between mainsail luff and clew show up in spite of the Cunningham having been set up hard, the mast bend must be reduced (for example, by increasing the mast control effect or reducing spreader sweep-back).

Due to the high rig tension generated by setting the jib halyard up hard, the headsail is trimmed very flat. In order to lower its centre of effort, the upper after region has to be opened. That is effected either by moving the sheet leads aft or upwards, or it may already have been achieved by the increase in the mast rake.

Both methods are standard practice; racing dinghies primarily use the latter. In both cases, frequent practice is the only way to guarantee finding the right setting every time. Time and time again, you have to look for a comparison with other boats. Once the optimum setting has been found, the appropriate places have to be marked.

The simplest way of opening the leech is undoubtedly to ease the sheet slightly. However, that has the disadvantage that the foot loosens at the same time and the sail bellies more — whereas for severe weather with relatively smooth water precisely the opposite would be right. The foot must always remain stretched hard. The above-mentioned, somewhat fuller trim can be advantageous in an unpleasant seaway, but it does mean accepting that the boat will not point so well — the difference can amount to some five to seven degrees.

A criterion for the correct openness of the leech in the case of the Genoa is also the backwinded part of the mainsail. If this is too large and extends over half the sail area, the leech is closed too far. If on the other hand no backwinding is visible and the upper part of the headsail is slatting violently, then the leech has to be closed more. If now in spite of being trimmed properly the dinghy cannot be kept upright any longer, the traveller must be set to leeward or the mainsheet eased. Where dinghies have extensively overlapping Genoas, the backwind from the headsail will probably mean that the traveller cannot be moved all the way to leeward, because that wind striking the mainsail on its leeward side will push it back.

When it is about in line with the deck edge, the boom end will be shaken to and fro. If that happens, the Genoa sheet also must be eased. Sailing a dinghy upright in severe weather is made significantly easier by raising the centreboard up to about a quarter. This reduces the total pressure on it; the boat does not stagger so fiercely, and is generally better able to fall off to leeward. The heeling moment is reduced. What you lose by not pointing so well is more than made up by the increase in speed (due to the reduced heel).

Reaching

For as long as the dinghy remains safe to handle, the mainsail can be set full and with the leech closed. The handling of the mainsheet — and also the foresheet — is now decisive in preventing a capsize. This test of nerves can have the edge taken off it by opening the mainsail leech a little, namely by easing the kicking strap which reduces the wind pressure on the upper part of the sail. Gusts are more easily parried. However, if the wind moves aft the strap has to be set up again to avoid the boat yawing.

Watch out! If the strap has been set up really hard for beating, it must be eased somewhat before bearing away onto a reach or a run. Otherwise the tension on it may become excessive and the boom will break.

Ordering a New Mainsail

The cut of the mainsail is decisive for a boat's sailing characteristics. To cut a sail well, the sailmaker must be given extensive information about the rig.

The more a mast is bent in the fore and aft direction (i.e. the head is angled towards the stern), the flatter the mainsail can be trimmed. The sail camber thus depends on the mast bend; the proper distribution of the camber on the bend characteristic. Some masts bend predominantly in the upper part, some in the lower, so the sailmaker must know what the mast-bend curve looks like when cutting a mainsail, to allow him to match the luff round, and thereby the camber, to that curve.

Establishing such a mast-bend curve could not be easier. First of all the mast is bent as far as possible, using all available trimming facilities. Next the main halyard shackle is hooked onto the gooseneck (for'd end of the main boom) and the halyard set up hard. That halyard now forms the chord of the mast-bend curve. Using a bosun's chair and a foot-rule, the horizontal distances between the mast after edge (groove) and the taut halyard are measured — at vertical intervals of about two metres along the mast will do. The readings are recorded, on a graph and this is given to the sailmaker when ordering the sail.

But there is other information that is also useful to the sailmaker:

- boat type (length, beam, weight)
- boat's stability characteristic (ballast share)
- waters on which it is intended to sail
- prevailing wind-strengths there
- advice regarding class rules
- sail measurements along edges.

Trimming for Masthead Rig

Beat	little wind force 1–2		moderate wind force 3–4		stronger winds force 5–7	
	smooth water	rippled water	small waves	waves	small waves	rough water
Mast						
Upper shrouds	tight	tight	tight	tight	tight	v tight
Fore lowers	loose	loose	tensioned	loose	tight	v tight
Aft lowers	loose	loose	slack	loose	slack	looser
Backstay	loose	loose	taut	mod tight	tight	v tight
Mast bend	straight	straight	slight bend	almost straight	max bend	bend
Mainsail						
Luff	loose	loose	taut	almost tight	v tight	tight
Foot	loose	loose	taut	loosen	v tight	tight
Leech	slightly open	open	closed	slightly open	almost open	open
Sheet	eased	eased	tight	tight	v tight	tight
Kicking strap	loose	loose	tensioned	almost slack	tensioned	slightly slack
Traveller	to windward	to windward	amidships	amidships	to leeward	to leeward
Headsail						
Luff	loose	loose	tensioned	fairly taut	v tight	v tight
Sheet	eased	eased	tight	taut	v tight	tight
Sheet lead	forward	forward	normal	normal	normal/aft	normal
W/Ward TT	horizontal	horizontal	approx 30°	approx 20°	approx 70°	approx 60°
L/Ward TT	horizontal	horizontal	horizontal	horizontal	horizontal	horizontal

Trim for Masthead Rig

Reach		little wind force 1–2		moderate wind force 3–4		stronger winds force 5–7	
		smooth water	rippled water	small waves	waves	small waves	rough water
Mast	Upper shrouds	tight	tight	tight	v tight	v tight	v tight
	Fore lowers	slack	slack	loose	loose	taut	taut
	Aft lowers	tight	tight	taut	taut	looser	looser
	Backstay	slack	slack	loose	loose	taut	taut
	Mast bend	negative bend	negative bend	straight	straight	almost straight	almost straight
Mainsail	Luff	slack	slack	slack	slack	loose	loose
	Foot	slack	slack	slack	slack	loose	loose
	Leech	closed	closed	closed	almost closed	open little	open little
	Kicking strap	tensioned	slight tension	tight	tight	v tight	v tight
	Traveller	NA	NA	to leeward	to leeward	extreme leeward	extreme leeward
Headsail	Luff	slack	slack	slack	slack	loose	loose
	Sheet lead	outboard/for'd	outboard/for'd	outboard/for'd	outboard/for'd	outboard/for'd	outboard/for'd
	W/Ward TT	horizontal	horizontal	horizontal	horizontal	horizontal	horizontal
	L/Ward TT	horizontal	horizontal	horizontal	horizontal	horizontal	horizontal

Trim for Fractional Rig with Swept Spreaders

Beat		little wind force 1–2		moderate wind force 3–4		stronger winds force 5–7	
		smooth water	rippled water	small waves	waves	small waves	rough water
Mast	Upper shrouds	v tight	v tight	v tight	v tight	v tight	v tight
	Lowers shrouds	taut	v tight	slightly slack	slightly slack	max slack	loose
	Backstay	max slack	loose	slightly tight	tight	v tight	v tight
	Mast bend	straight	straight	slight bend	fair bend	max bend	max bend
Mainsail	Luff	loose	very slack	taut	taut	v tight	tight
	Foot	loose	very loose	tensioned	taut	v tight	tight
	Leech	open	fairly open	almost closed	closed	open	almost open
	Sheet	eased	eased	taut	taut	v tight	v tight
	Kicking strap	loose	loose	taut	taut	v tight	v tight
	Traveller	to windward	to windward	amidships	amidships	to leeward	to leeward
Headsail	Luff	slack	very loose	taut	almost taut	v tight	v tight
	Sheet	eased	eased	v tight	tight	v tight	tight
	Sheet lead	forward	forward	normal	normal	normal/astern	normal
	W/Ward TT	horizontal	horizontal	approx 30°	approx 20°	approx 70°	approx 60°
	L/Ward TT	horizontal	horizontal	horizontal	horizontal	horizontal	horizontal

Trim for Fractional Rig with Swept Spreaders

Reach		little wind force 1–2		moderate wind force 3–4		stronger winds force 5–7	
		smooth water	rippled water	small waves	waves	small waves	rough water
Mast	Upper shrouds	v tight	v tight	v tight	v tight	v tight	v tight
	Lower shrouds	v tight	v tight	v tight	v tight	tight	tight
	Backstay	slack	slack	loose	loose	max slack	max slack
	Mast bend	straight	straight	straight	straight	slight bend	slight bend
Mainsail	Luff	slack	slack	slack	slack	almost slack	almost slack
	Foot	slack	slack	slack	slack	almost slack	almost slack
	Leech	closed	closed	closed	closed	almost closed	almost closed
	Kicking strap	tensioned	tensioned	tight	tight	v tight	v tight
	Traveller	NA	NA	to leeward	to leeward	to leeward	to leeward
Headsail	Luff	slack	slack	slack	slack	slight tension	slight tension
	Sheet lead	forward	forward	outboard/for'd	outboard/for'd	outboard/for'd	outboard/for'd
	W/Ward TT	horizontal	horizontal	horizontal	horizontal	horizontal	horizontal
	L/Ward TT	horizontal	horizontal	horizontal	horizontal	horizontal	horizontal

Trim for Fractional Rig with Running Backstays

Beat		little wind force 1–2		moderate wind force 3–4		stronger winds force 5–7	
		smooth water	rippled water	small waves	waves	small waves	rough water
Mast	Upper shrouds	v tight	v tight	v tight	v tight	v tight	v tight
	Lower shrouds	v tight	v tight	v tight	v tight	v tight	v tight
	W/ward runner	taut	taut	slight tight	tight	v tight	v tight
	Backstay	slack	slack	rod tension	tight	v tight	v tight
	Mast bend	straight	straight	s ight bend	bend	max bend	max bend
Mainsail	Luff	loose	slack	taut	taut	v tight	tight
	Foot	loose	slack	taut	moderate tight	v tight	tight
	Leech	open	slightly open	almost closed	a little open	open	almost open
	Sheet	eased	eased	t ght	tight	tight	v tight
	Kicking strap	eased	eased	t ght	tight	v tight	v tight
	Traveller	to w/ward	to w/ward	amidships	amidships	to leeward	to leeward
Headsail	Luff	loose	slack	taut	taut	v tight	v tight
	Sheet	eased	eased	tight	tight	v tight	v tight
	Sheet lead	forward	forward	normal	normal	normal/astern	normal
	W/Ward TT	horizontal	horizontal	about 30°	about 20°	about 70°	about 60°
	L/Ward TT	horizontal	horizontal	horizontal	horizontal	horizontal	horizontal

Trim for Fractional Rig with Running Backstays

Reach		little wind force 1-2		moderate wind force 3-4		stronger winds force 5-7	
		smooth water	rippled water	small waves	waves	small waves	rough water
Mast	Upper shrouds	v tight	v tight	v tight	v tight	v tight	v tight
	Lower shrouds	v tight	v tight	v tight	v tight	v tight	v tight
	W/ward runner	slightly eased	slightly eased	slight tension	slight tension	taut	taut
	Backstay	slack	slack	slack	slack	taut	taut
	Mast bend	upright	upright	upright	upright	some bend	some bend
Mainsail	Luff	loose	loose	loose	loose	slight tension	slight tension
	Foot	loose	loose	loose	loose	slight tension	slight tension
	Leech	closed	closed	closed	closed	open little	almost closed
	Kicking strap	slight tension	slight tension	tight	tight	v tight	v tight
	Traveller	NA	NA	to leeward	to leeward	to leeward	to leeward
Headsail	Luff	loose	loose	loose	loose	slight tension	slight tension
	Sheet lead	for'd	for'd	for'd/outboard	for'd/outboard	for'd/outboard	for'd/outboard
	W/Ward TT	horizontal	horizontal	horizontal	horizontal	horizontal	horizontal
	L/Ward TT	horizontal	horizontal	horizontal	horizontal	horizontal	horizontal

Sail Trim Tables

Trim for Dinghy Rig

	Beat	little wind force 1–2		moderate wind force 3–4		stronger winds force 5–7	
		smooth water	rippled water	small waves	waves	small waves	rough water
Mast	Upper shrouds/Forestay	taut	taut	v tight	v tight	v tight	v tight
	Maststay	max tight	max tight	neutral	neutral	max loose	max loose
	Spreader angle	slight	slight	medium	medium	max	max
	Kicking strap	loose	loose	tension	tension	tight	tight
	Mast bend	upright	upright	little bend	increased bend	max bend	max bend
Mainsail	Luff	loose	loose	slight tension	looser	v tight	tight
	Foot	loose	loose	slight tension	looser	v tight	tight
	Leech	slightly open	slightly open	closed	slightly closed	open	almost open
	Sheet tension	eased	max ease	v tight	tight	tight	slightly eased
	Traveller	to windward	to windward	amidships	amidships	to leeward	to leeward
Headsail	Luff	loose	loose	taut	taut	tight	taut
	Leech	closed	closed	closed	almost closed	open	almost open
	Sheet tension	eased	max eased	v tight	tight	v tight	tight
	Sheet lead	for'd	for'd	neutral	neutral	aft	aft
	W/Ward TT	horizontal	horizontal	approx 30°	approx 20°	approx 70°	approx 60°
	L/Ward TT	horizontal	horizontal	horizontal	horizontal	horizontal	horizontal

Trim for Dinghy Rig

Reach		little wind force 1–2		moderate wind force 3–4		stronger winds force 5–7	
		smooth water	rippled water	small waves	waves	small waves	rough water
Mast	Upper shrouds/Forestay	loose	loose	tight	tight	tight	tight
	Maststay	max tight	max tight	max tight	max tight	tight	tight
	Spreader angle	slight	slight	slight	slight	medium	medium
	Kicking strap	taut	taut	tight	tight	v tight	v tight
	Mast bend	upright	upright	upright	upright	slight bend	slight bend
Mainsail	Luff	loose	loose	loose	loose	tension	tension
	Foot	loose	loose	loose	loose	tension	tension
	Leech	closed	almost closed	closed	closed	almost open	open
	Traveller	NA	NA	to leeward	to leeward	to leeward	to leeward
Headsail	Luff	loose	loose	loose	loose	tensioned	tensioned
	Leech	closed	closed	closed	closed	slightly open	slightly open
	Sheet lead	for'd	for'd	for'd/outboard	for'd/outboard	for'd/outboard	for'd/outboard
	W/Ward TT	horizontal	horizontal	horizontal	horizontal	horizontal	horizontal
	L/Ward TT	horizontal	horizontal	horizontal	horizontal	horizontal	horizontal

Index

aback 75
angle, spreader 105

baby stay 84
backstay 12
  running 66
  standing 66
  tensioner 86
barber hauler 55,77
batten 36,73
beating 72,88,93,94,100–
  102,111,112
bend, mast 105
block 14,21

camber 28,45,56,61,63,72,73,
  74,78,100,103,116
  depth 33
centre of effort 68
chainplate 84,92,97
cleat 13,98
clew outhaul 28,76
control, mast 107
Cunningham 103

dinghy rig 103

eyelet, reefing 31

flow, turbulent 31,37,65
foot 60
  tension 28
forestay 42,66,74,84,88

Genoa 70,73,76,77,81,88,111,114
gooseneck 15,98,107

halyard 13
  headsail 42
  main 17
headsail 42,73,74,76,79,81,82,110
  roller-reefing 52
  window 57
heel 75,94,110
heel, leeward 72
helm, neutral 68
  weather
    17,26,31,52,67,68,75,86,94
hull speed 61,62

jib 77

Kevlar 19
kicking strap
  12,20,41,69,73,79,80,98,104,
  106
knife 11

lead, sheet 46,77
leech, flutter 33,60
  line 33,60,81,82
  mainsail 33
  tell-tales 36
length, spreader 105
lower shrouds 88
luff, mainsail 27,38
  tension 27,28,42
  tensioner (Cunningham)
    26,76,103

mainsail 17,73,74,75,78,79,80,81,
  82,103,111,116
mainsheet 104,110

mast 65,91,99,110
  bend 31,103,116
  bend curve 116
  compression fracture 89
  control 104
  deck-mounted 98
  gate 98
  heel 110
  keel-stepped 98–99
  rake 46,52,68,86,101
  section 98,104
  struts 107
  trim 78,86
masthead rig 84
muscle box 24

pointing 73
points, reef 30
pre-bend, mast 92,113

rake 64,91,110
reaching 78,88,93,94,101,102,112
reef 30,70,76,102
  flattening 29
rig tension 104
rigging screw 15,86
running 81
running backstays
  92,96,97,98,100

sailcloth 48,77
self-tacking jib 54
seven-eighths rig 84,90
shackle 13
sheave, diameter 20

sheet, lead 52,73,83
  leech 31
  lightweight 73
  main 12,31
  primary 12
shroud 66,92
  aft lower 84
  fore lower 84
  lower 97
  upper 84,97
slider 17
spinnaker 82
spreaders
  15,86,91,97,104,105,113
spreader – length 105
standing backstay 84
swept-back spreaders 90

tell-tales 21,33,57
tension – foot 81
  forestay 42,86
  leech 81
toggle 66
topping lift 38
traveller 12,14,31,39,74,76,79
turbulence 57
twist 33,39,69,70,81

weather helm
  17,26,31,52,67,68,75,86,94
winch 14
wire, galvanised 19
  stainless 19

yaw 82